BETWEEN
TWO WORLDS

JOSEPH GELEPLAY'S FIGHT FOR
EDUCATION IN LIBERIA

Victoria Gebeplay Corlon

BETWEEN TWO WORLDS

JOSEPH GELEPLAY'S FIGHT FOR EDUCATION IN LIBERIA

Victoria Geleplay Corlon

Anointed Rose Press Publishing

iii

Anointed Rose Press™

The Anointed Rose Press name and logo are registered Trademarks of
ANOINTED ROSE PRESS

BETWEEN TWO WORLDS©
"Joseph Geleplay's Fight for Education in Liberia"

Between Two World's/Victoria Geleplay Corlon
(trade hardcover: alkaline paper)

ISBN 13:978-0-9896110-2-2
LCCN: 2025911341

1. Biography   2. Personal Memoir

The Cover Design: Anointed Rose Press
(484)378-0939

Anointed Rose Press Publisher
Email: septembersummer09@gmail.com
www.september-summer.com

USA

CONTENTS

ACKNOWLEDGMENTS ||

There are so many people that I am grateful to for helping me tell my dad's story. I want to begin with my beloved husband, Wilfred Corlon Sr. Your unwavering support and love have been the foundation of our lives together. Throughout our 30.5 years of marriage, you have not only stood by me but have truly made my challenges your own. When you married me, you embraced my entire family with open arms and a kind heart. I cannot imagine navigating this vast and sometimes overwhelming world without you by my side. To our wonderful boys, Wilfred Jr. and Vatekeh, thank you for being the light of my life. Being your mother is the greatest honor I could ever ask for, and I am endlessly proud of the men you are becoming. My heart is full of love and gratitude to my mother, Mabel Warner Geleplay, for the countless sacrifices and hardships she endured for the wellbeing of her children and family. From an early age, she exemplified hard work and compassion, instilling these values deeply within me. Her unwavering dedication and love have profoundly shaped the person I am today.

To my beloved sisters Joan, Ethel, and Bertha, words cannot fully express my gratitude for your support and invaluable contributions to this project. Your deep wells of knowledge about Kanweaken, your patience with my endless questions, and your willingness to share your cherished memories have been instrumental in bringing this work to life. Your dedication, not only in sharing your experiences, but also in reaching out to others and conducting research has enriched this journey in ways I could never have imagined. Again, a special thank you to Sister Joan whose generosity extended even further by taking the time to translate Grebo phrases into English. Your effort has been a bridge, helping to preserve and share our culture with a wider audience, ensuring that the beauty of our language and traditions lives on.

To my sister Esther Geleplay in Liberia, your help in gathering and confirming the names of our family members has been a gift beyond measure. Your connection to our roots and your willingness to assist in piecing together our family history has brought clarity to this project. To my sister Florence, THANK YOU, THANK YOU, THANK YOU for watching over me.

To my nephew Nabieu Turay in Sierra Leone, thank you so much for sharing your wonderful experience in Liberia. It truly warmed my heart to hear about your interaction with the stranger who was excited to talk to you just from hearing your grandfather's name. Moments like these are a beautiful reminder of the lasting impact he has had on those around him and how deeply he is remembered and respected. To all my brothers, nephews, nieces, aunties, uncles, and cousins, each of you has played a vital role in my life. Your love and affection have been a constant source of strength, and I am truly grateful for the warmth you bring to every moment we share. A special thank you to Uncle Fred Slobert for sharing your recollections. They are treasures that bridge the past with the present, allowing us to see where we've come from and how far we've grown.

To Jim and Cheryl Newton, thank you for being a part of my journey by wrapping your strong arms around a scared young girl. To Richard Bowen, thank you for unhesitatingly being a source. To my friends, thank you for the laughter we've shared, the lessons we've learned, and the memories we continue to create. This journey would not have been possible without my village.

AUTHOR'S NOTE ||

This is the story of my father, which extends far beyond him as an individual. He fathered 27 children, and his descendants now live across two continents, though many remain in Liberia where our story began.

As I've worked to document our family history, I've encountered both successes and frustrations. Some relatives I could only identify by name, with no other details about their lives. Others I knew existed but couldn't be located with phone numbers that no longer worked or addresses where they no longer lived. Many times, I felt discouraged by these gaps in our family record.

But I came to understand that capturing every detail wasn't the point. What matters is remembering our shared heritage and maintaining the connections we do have, however scattered we may be. The relatives I couldn't find are still part of our story.

Our family includes people from all walks of life – teachers, artists, engineers, healthcare workers, farmers, and more. Each of us carries forward some aspect of my father's character and determination. As I write this, I'm struck by both the size of our family and the intimacy of our bonds. Though we're separated by great distances, we remain connected through the legacy of a man who put family above all else.

To all who share our father's legacy, whether I know you or not, you matter. You are irreplaceable parts of who we are as a family. Distance may separate us, but it cannot break the ties that bind us together.

...*Victoria Geleplay-Corlon*

ENDORSEMENT ||

In her new book, Mrs. Victoria Geleplay-Corlon adeptly narrates the story of her father, a schoolteacher from a small town in Liberia, Kanweaken, and the intricate dance he faced between local tradition and his unwavering passion for education.

Mr. Geleplay is portrayed as a man of vision and steadfast optimism who inspired not only the people of Kanweaken as a dedicated teacher, but also the members of the national legislature of Liberia when he served in the House of Representatives.

Teacher Geleplay believed in his people, even amidst betrayal and challenges. Teacher Geleplay's conviction that tradition and progress should walk hand in hand and that education is the key to enlightenment - is a powerful message that resonates now and for generations to come.

...Saye Gbalazeh

Assistant Professor of Law
University of Liberia

ENDORSEMENT ||

BETWEEN TWO WORLDS offers a rare glimpse into the culture and history of the region around the town of Gbeapo Kanweaken, in Southeastern Liberia. As a Peace Corps volunteer in Liberia from 1985-86, I taught at Gbeapo Central High School in Kanweaken and worked on projects involving many other schools in the region.

Reading Ms. Corlon's story not only immersed me once again in the beauty and challenges of that era, but also made me realize that that I might never have had those enriching experiences if Joseph Geleplay had not promoted the advancement of education in the region as he did.

…Richard Bowen

Director of Software Development
Xperi Inc
NC, USA

PROLOGUE |

Despite the sweltering heat that pressed down on us that day, the gathering in front of our family home in Kanweaken spilled onto the street. Hundreds of people had come to honor my father—his siblings, children, grandchildren, former students, and countless others whose lives he had touched.

I couldn't stop staring at the grave they had dug right there in our front yard. That wasn't how things were normally done here. Everyone else who had died was buried in the cemetery outside of town. But the elders had insisted that my father would rest here, at the heart of the community he'd served his whole life; where everyone who passed by would see his grave and be reminded of all he'd done for this town and for all the people of Liberia.

Out of habit, I glanced toward the place where my father used to like to stand after dinner . . . and froze. I knew he was dead, but there, standing in that place where I'd seen my father countless times, was my uncle Elijah, his older brother. I could have sworn it was Dad. My legs gave out, and I crumpled to the ground. Uncle Elijah was there in an instant, scooping me up. "I know, I know," he murmured. We didn't need to say more.

The rest of the day passed in a blur of familiar faces. I embraced the family members who were still living, and we reminisced about those who were gone. My father's siblings included Uncle Elijah, who had three known children, two who passed away when I was a child. His daughter Caroline passed away in 2023 and is survived by five children and four grandchildren.

Then there was Uncle Phillip Dweah Geleplay, my dad's younger brother, who was respected in his own right. He was a man of few words, but very hard working, and who made sure that his family were taken care of. He also had five children, three deceased and two alive, and eight grandchildren.

Aunt Betty Wleoh Geleplay had four children—two deceased, two alive, and four grandchildren. Then there was Ida Snoh Geleplay, Aunty Ida, whom I remember very well, had ten children. Three are now deceased and seven are still alive, along with nineteen grandchildren and one great-great grandchild. Tall and slender, with fair skin, she looked the same year after year. Talk about timeless beauty. Her son Moses Juwillie, whom I'm very close to, has her good genes.

And finally, there was Phebe Potie Geleplay. Aunty Phebe was the only member of the Geleplay family who went to college. She is survived by four children, fourteen grandchildren, and four great grandchildren. The last of Joseph's siblings died shortly after he was born.

Relatives I hadn't seen in years had memories to share, and I couldn't get enough of the stories they told about my dad. I heard about his relentless curiosity as a little boy, and his lifelong passion for education as a way forward for his community. His students, many of whom I hadn't met until then, spoke of his courage as he found peaceful ways to navigate the violent clashes between traditional customs and Western ways during a chaotic time of desperate hopes and great losses.

My father spent six years teaching the youth of Kanweaken to read and write before he started getting a paycheck. He taught the children of Liberia, in and out of school, for a total of thirty-seven years. Beyond his role as a teacher, he was also a translator, nurse, tailor, hunter, carpenter, businessman, captain in militia drills, and finally a congressman in Liberia's national government. His death, following a stroke at the age of sixty-three, was a sad ending for a patriot and warrior who had devoted his entire life to making life in his village and his country better for everyone.

My aching heart found comfort in the words shared by family members, old friends, and students. Dad had a way of making each person feel like they were the most special one in the room. He impacted so many lives in so many ways.

Early one morning, unable to sleep, I slipped out for a walk. Kanweaken had changed so much since I had left more than a decade before when I had gone to live with my older sister Florence in Monrovia at the age of seven. Monrovia had better schools, and my dad wanted me to get a good start in life.

Now, a proper high school stood where there had once been empty land—my father's dream realized. New houses, filled with people from other parts of Liberia and even neighboring countries, dotted the landscape. The old open area where people used to trade farm produce and other goods had become an official farmer's market, complete with a large, covered pavilion for the rainy seasons.

Yet some things in this town remained familiar. Papaya trees still grew in the back of our house, their fruit hanging heavy. The air still smelled of smoked and dried meat and palm butter stew. The people still moved with unhurried grace and wore the open smiles I remembered from childhood. Standing there, I thought about how different this town was from the village my father had been born into back in 1919.

01 | 📚JG

KANWEAKEN

Kanweaken was a small cluster of mud-walled, thatch-roofed houses, home to maybe one hundred people, when my father was born. Deep in the hinterlands of Liberia, it was only connected to other villages by walking paths through the dense rainforest. The nearest churches and schools, novelties still unseen by the villagers of Kanweaken, had been constructed in southern Liberia's port city, Harper, about a four days' walk from the village.

Further up the coast, in far off Monrovia, descendants of former American slaves had elected their sixteenth president, Daniel Edward Howard, continuing a government closely modeled after the one they had left behind in the United States. After bloodshed and negotiations with coastal tribes, the settlers established their communities. They built schools, churches, and homes that reflected their

American heritage. They wore Western clothing, spoke English, and practiced Christianity.

The antics of these "Congo people" were little more than a worrisome rumor to the people of Kanweaken. Farmers and hunters, warriors when the necessity arose, still lived by rhythms that were dictated by nature and steeped in tradition. It would have been surprising if President Howard's name was ever uttered in a village so deep in the jungles.

It wasn't until 1931 that the first Western missionaries appeared in Kanweaken, riding tall in hammocks carried by young men because they didn't have the stamina or skills to walk safely through the dense jungles. According to one missionary who traveled extensively from village to village by hammock, the rugged trails were frequently crossed by snakes and other dangerous creatures, and sometimes so overgrown that a person could only crawl through the vines and brush if they weren't wielding a machete.

Joseph, like any other child, learned to walk through the jungle on his own two legs as soon as a younger sibling was born to occupy his place on his mother's back. His father, Nyeneh Geleplay (later called Jimmy by the missionaries), and his mother, Kpaweh (who would become Catherine), were farmers, as were most of the people in Kanweaken and the surrounding villages. Farming took up most of their days, no matter what the season. Planting was done during the rainy season from April to October. Families worked through occasional downpours, the humidity dripping from their skin. The dry season, from November to April, was when farmers harvested their crops. The hot sun beat down on them as they worked.

If a man had more than one wife, which was always the case, each woman in turn had her husband's help on the farm, and then he would spend that night with her. Some families joined forces to work. All of a man's wives and children would spend a few days to a week on wife number one's farm, then the next week on wife number two's farm, and so forth. If for any reason a woman had a problem with this arrangement, she was on her own.

Each morning at dawn, the family made their way from the dense cluster of village huts to the patch of land Joseph's mother had chosen, and his father had cleared. There, they grew rice, cassava, and other crops. The narrow paths would have been wet with morning dew, and lined with high bushes and leaves that brushed against their shoulders and swatted their legs as they walked.

Joseph walked single file behind his older brother, Elijah, and ahead of his younger brother, Philip. The children walked between their parents. His younger sisters each took their turn being carried on his mother's back as they were born, sharing space with whatever provisions the family needed for the day. Tools were left on the farm rather than carried back and forth.

This was the way families always traveled—the husband leading the way, children in the middle, and the wife bringing up the rear. This formation protected the children from any dangers that might lie ahead or behind. As the day progressed, their tasks shifted. The children might help gather wood for cooking and heating water, or they might go to the river to fish or bathe.

In the evenings, the family would return home to the village, their bodies tired but their spirits strong. Some women preferred to cook dinner on the farm and take it home, and others, like Joseph's mother, preferred to get home before cooking. The adults gathered with neighbors for moonlight storytelling while waiting to get sleepy. Teens stole away by twos to flirt and make promises for the future. Boys and girls played hide and seek until exhausted or they started to quarrel. Many things happened during those nights that only the darkness knows.

As Joseph got older, he and his brothers were taken into the jungle for secret initiation rites by the Poro society, an organization that trained young boys for manhood. No one ever talked about what those rites entailed or who participated in them. These were sometimes harrowing tests on the way to manhood that not every boy survived.

This was the world into which Joseph was born—a world of close-knit community, hard work, and deep connection to the land. Almost everything about this life would soon change.

It was the dry season of 1928—Joseph was nine years old—when an anthropologist named George Schwab and his wife walked into the village on an expedition funded by the Firestone Tire Company. Firestone was blatantly looking to expand their labor force at the rubber plantation where they had broken ground two years prior.

Schwab looked inside mouths, measured crania, and pinched biceps. He noted that the Half-Grebo, as he mistakenly labeled the inland Grebo tribe that our family belongs to, were "the most self-confident, reserved in manner, and dignified in bearing. . . . The children were obedient, respectful, quiet, and industrious" (Schwab, 1947, p. 451).

In nearby Palipo, the anthropologist met people who, when they were instructed to either build a road or pay a hefty fine, chose to pay the fine, even though this expense meant going hungry (Schwab, 1947, p. 451). Schwab wrote, "The Liberian Hinterland has at last been drawn into the stream of rapidly changing conditions affecting the rest of primitive Africa" (Schwab, 1947, p. ix).

But ten years later, a Harvard University map still sweepingly labeled the area "Unsurveyed" and "Sparsely Inhabited" (Harley, 1938). Even missionaries, the first White faces many indigenous people saw, didn't arrive in Kanweaken until 1931. My father was twelve years old when a young Pentecostal couple named Philip and Grace Elsea came into Kanweaken, singing and praising as the hammock bearers carried them into the village clearing.

Prior to the missionaries' arrival, the village elders had to carefully consider the invitation they extended. They had heard mostly positive accounts of others like them who lived in neighboring villages. Hosting missionaries, with their medicines, magic, and stories, had brought these other villages a certain amount of prestige that some people in Kanweaken envied. Bible magic was reportedly quite powerful, and the missionaries seemed eager to share it. Some hoped it might help protect them from the Congo government that had been making life increasingly difficult for Grebo communities closer to the coast. Visitors who came to Kanweaken to trade had been bringing alarming news lately about the Congos violently enforcing labor and imposing severe taxes that left entire villages unable to feed their families.

It is worth noting that, in the elders' discussions, the missionaries spoke the same language and came from the same country as the Congo government that had been the cause of all the trouble in the first place. So, could they reasonably be expected to do more good than harm? After several nights of deliberation around the evening fire, the elders decided to send six young men to the coast, a place most Kanweaken villagers had never seen, to escort the Elseas to Kanweaken.

I can imagine how eagerly young Joseph awaited the decision of the elders and then waited for the missionaries to arrive. He was driven by a lifelong sense of curiosity. As soon as he ever heard about anything that piqued his interest, he had to experience it firsthand. He must have heard stories about missionaries and their strange ways from travelers who came to the market in Kanweaken. He had once seen a book, a proud possession his neighbor had traded for, and he marveled at how those little black marks could contain information. The prospect of learning this new kind of magic filled him with excitement; and now, Kanweaken was receiving missionaries of their very own!

The whole village buzzed with anticipation and worry for the fifteen days the young men were gone. *Why were they taking so long?* It should only have been an eight-day journey there and back.

Finally, just as rain clouds were starting to gather at the end of a long dry season, a messenger came to Kanweaken shouting that the missionaries were close. There were, of course, no telephones in the hinterlands of Liberia, so messengers like this were the usual means by which the village learned about what was going on in the surrounding area.

Each type of message was delivered with a distinctive tone that gave the people a general idea of what was happening. When they heard, "*I waayah ooooooo,*" for example, all of the women and girls and every boy who had not yet been inducted into the Poro Society would run into a house, whether it was their own house or not. This message meant that Qwee was about to pass through—a powerful entity that could strike the uninitiated dead on sight.

On the day the missionaries arrived, Joseph stood with the other children, craning his neck to catch the first glimpse of the strangers, and trying to look brave like the adults. When the procession finally emerged from the forest path, Joseph's heart raced. There they were—two pale-skinned beings swaying in hammocks carried by the young men whose departure felt like ages ago instead of days.

The hammock bearers, animated despite their burden, called out jubilant greetings. The air filled with a mixture of Grebo exclamations, excited chatter, and the unfamiliar sounds of English. As the elders stepped forward to greet the foreigners, Joseph edged closer, eager to hear the unfamiliar sounds of the missionaries' language.

The day after the Elseas arrived, they both set to work helping to build a large hut for themselves on the edge of the village. Even though they were only two people, their house was larger than that of most families, and everyone seemed to think that was proper. Nobody would say that Kanweaken lacked hospitality.

Once the hut was complete, the Elseas quickly became part of the village life. Grace Elsea spent time with Joseph's mother and aunts. She seemed eager to learn what the various foods were called and how to prepare them. The women were not quite as interested in the tins and dried goods that Grace offered. They had seen such things at village markets before. But they politely accepted the gifts.

Everyone knew that missionaries did not farm, but it was still strange to see healthy young adults staying in the village all day. Philip spent much of his time staring at the pages of his books, then writing in other books. He used a complicated looking box made of wood, metal, and cloth that Joseph learned was a camera.

It was mostly children who sat at Philip Elsea's feet as he told story after fantastical story. The mango tree's broad leaves cast dappled shadows over the missionary and his young students as his resonant voice carried across the clearing. He would throw up his hands and shout, "Holy! Holy God!" whenever he got to a point in the story where something good was about to happen. His sweat-soaked hair stuck to his forehead, and his blue eyes would flash.

The translator who had come from the coast with the Elseas spoke a different dialect of the Grebo language, but he kept up pretty well. It wasn't long before Joseph was able to follow the stories in English on his own. Most of the younger kids quickly picked up English too, and they delighted in this new way to keep secrets from their parents.

Joseph and his friend Marcy, both twelve, were worlds apart in their approach to these new teachings. While Joseph's mind analyzed the meaning of the words, Marcy seemed to vibrate with spiritual energy as he listened, his eyes shining as if reflecting some unseen light.

At the crescendo of the lesson Philip was teaching, he exclaimed, "And Jesus commanded his disciples, "Go into all the world and preach the gospel to all creation.""

"Teacher!" Joseph interrupted. "You said Jesus was already dead? And then he went up into the sky? How could they hear him?"

Philip's face softened. "The disciples felt His words in their hearts, Joseph. It changed them forever."

"I feel the words!" Marcy said. "Yes, Jesus! I feel them in my *heart*!"

Philip looked at Joseph's puzzled expression. "You have to come down from here . . .", as he tapped his head, "and in here . . .", as he tapped his chest.

"But how do we know?" Joseph asked. "How do we know that's really what Jesus really said . . . in their hearts?"

A knowing smile played on Philip's lips. "An excellent question, Joseph. The teachings were carefully written down by His followers." He lifted the thick black book he always carried. "That's the origin of the Scripture we study today."

The boys' distinct natures became ever more apparent as their education progressed. Joseph scratched out new vocabulary in the dirt, his methodical mind working to connect these novel concepts with his existing knowledge. Marcy, by contrast, seemed to absorb the teachings through his very skin, swaying slightly as if moved by an invisible breeze when the missionaries taught.

As they walked home from their predawn Bible lessons one morning, Marcy's exuberance spilled over into spontaneous hymns. Joseph walked alongside him in contemplative silence, watching streaks of tender golden light appear between the trees.

At Marcy's mother's hut, a child's cry pierced the evening calm. His baby sister, Mabel, barely three years old, toddled out, her face streaked with tears. Marcy scooped her up with practiced ease, soothing her with his singing.

The scene stirred something in Joseph—a sense of the interconnectedness of their lives, of the web of relationships that shaped their community. Scholar and preacher, sister and brother, teacher and student— all part of something larger than any one of them could fully comprehend.

Some of the elders were amused by the missionaries. On the whole, the older generations were wary but tolerant and polite. News continued to come in of battles raging in places it would only take a few days to walk to, where their kinsmen were standing firm against the fledgling Liberian government. They quietly wondered whose side the missionaries would take if the fight came to Kanweaken.

Both of the missionaries laughed a lot, and more at themselves than anyone else. They were quick to apologize, saying *tetah* in their funny accents whenever they made a mistake. They were hard not to like.

Joseph's father, Jimmy, noticing his son's keen interest in the newcomers, offered a gentle warning.

"It's the blow," he said softly, his cool breath tickling the back of Joseph's hand, "after the bite!" There was a sudden flash of teeth, and Jimmy laughed as Joseph jerked his hand back. "Stay alert, son," he said. His smile was playful, but his tone was serious.

Joseph understood the bite and the blow his father was talking about. The Congo government had tried to conquer his people by restricting their trade and heavily taxing the food they produced. They forced them to build roads, not for their own use, but for even more foreigners who came to mine precious minerals from the land and to harvest rubber. When villages banded together and fought back, the government tried to conquer them by force. That was the bite.

The Grebo and Kru tribes had survived the bite. Would they succumb to the cooling breath of these missionaries who brought food and medicine, promising that everything would work out in the end— as long as the people were willing to wait patiently for heaven?

Joseph wanted to believe heaven would be nice, but when he closed his eyes and tried to imagine it, all he saw were the clear-water streams where he and his brothers swam, especially the wide, bubbling creek called Klee. Certain parts of this creek had shallow depths of fast, turbulent water, and there was a natural pool in the shape of a rectangle. It was said that a magical being lived in the pool, so no one could get in there. This was where the young folks socialized while fetching water and washing clothes. There was always so much rice to pound. It was supposed to be a girl's job, but sometimes Joseph and his brothers helped with it.

The Klee was nature at its best. Why would anyone be content to wait for the Christian heaven when there was such a nice, wide walking path down to the Klee?

Joseph and his younger brother Philip were playing near the edge of the village when they heard a commotion. Curious, Joseph ran toward the sound, only to find a group of elders surrounding Grace Elsea. The missionary woman stood near the sacred juju house, a place strictly off-limits to women and outsiders, and especially women who were outsiders.

"Did she go in there?" Joseph whispered to Philip.

Phillip widened his eyes and said nothing.

The boys saw their parents in the crowd and went to stand next to them.

Old Man Klubo's face was stern as he spoke to the translator. "Ask her why she has come to this forbidden place," he said. His voice was low, the way it always was during ceremonies.

The translator relayed the question, and Grace smiled. She spoke quickly, her hands gesturing. Joseph strained to understand.

The translator turned back to the elders. "She says she was curious and didn't realize this area was forbidden. She apologizes for her mistake."

A murmur ran through the gathered crowd. Joseph's mother shook her head disapprovingly. "How can she not know?" she whispered. "Even the smallest child knows not to go near the juju house."

Old Man Klubo's expression was serious. "Tell her," he said to the translator, "that this juju is powerful. It protects our village and ensures our future. But any woman who sees it will never bear children. This is why our women know to stay away."

Joseph watched Grace's face as she received this information. He expected to see fear or at least concern, but instead, the missionary woman continued to smile and nod. If anything, she seemed reassured! Did she not want children?

Grace spoke again, and the translator hesitated before turning back to the elders.

"She says she understands and respects our beliefs, but she also believes her God will protect her and bless her with children if that is His will."

The people exchanged glances and murmured. Joseph's father frowned and gripped Joseph's hand tightly.

Old Man Klubo spoke again. His voice was still grave, but it had softened. "We have welcomed you to our village, and we hope you will respect our ways. The power of the juju is not to be taken lightly. Please, do not come to this house again."

Grace nodded, but Joseph sensed a stubborn determination in her eyes. She was still smiling. As she turned to leave, escorted by the translator, Joseph heard his father mutter, "*A mie jeba.*" We shall see.

In the days and weeks that followed, Joseph noticed how the women of the village watched Grace with pity. What was a woman's life for if she couldn't have children, they wondered aloud. Grace had told them that she and Philip had only been married for a few years, so she should have had many fertile years ahead of her. The village women were certain that this good-natured woman had sealed her fate, and it was a sad thing to see.

Joseph took his father's warnings about the blow after the bite seriously, but as the weeks passed, he found himself drawn more and more to the wide world the missionaries talked about in their stories.

Jimmy, always the cautious one, tried to explain to his son, "That world is not open to you, Juty. They try to get you to become like them, but I think they would get mad if you were too much like them. See how these missionaries act when we have dances? They don't accept the world that made you, so how can they fully accept you?"

Kanweaken was known among the villages all around for its talented dancers. For major events like weddings and births, and sometimes simply for entertainment, the dancers could be counted upon to bring everyone together and remind them of how strong and proud their village was.

Thukloh was a ceremonial dance performed by men and women, usually after the death of an elder or something of significance. *Kpnami* was performed by boys during their initiation into the Poro society. Another dance called *Nyenewaleh* gave older women a way to express their feelings about life experiences.

Then there was *Combo,* a party dance where boys and girls tried their best to catch one another's eye. They would move with exaggerated swagger, hips swaying and shoulders shimmying. Some would call out flirtatious challenges, while others relied on meaningful glances and coy smiles. The bolder dancers would edge closer to their chosen partners, showing off their most impressive moves. It was a playful, charged atmosphere where budding romances often sparked. *Wayah* was another party dance, this one for old and young people alike.

Joseph never missed a dance. The Elseas never came out of their hut when any kind of dancing was going on. They said it had something to do with the Devil. Joseph didn't often question what they said, but this was one idea he just couldn't swallow.

The day came when the Elseas explained that their service was required in Harper City. Three years had gone by. "So quickly!" Grace shook her head. The whole village was sorry to see them go, but fifteen-year-old Joseph took it harder than anyone. They hadn't yet built the school Joseph and many of the other children were hoping for.

When would Kanweaken get another chance to start a school? Joseph could read now, and for what?

Almost all the books in Kanweaken would be leaving with the Elseas. Joseph was the one who helped pack them into wooden crates as the Elseas got ready for the trail.

The missionary put his hand on Joseph's arm when he was done. His blue eyes sparkled with either humor or kindness—it wasn't always easy to tell the difference. "How would you like to come with us to the coast?" Philip asked.

Joseph's heart leapt. He had been dreaming of this, but he never dared to hope he would actually be invited.

"You've picked up English so quickly. It's remarkable! We could get you into our school at Cape Palmas. Take you all the way up to the eighth grade. Imagine that!" Images raced through Joseph's mind as Philip spoke.

"You could be like John, our translator. Travel with missionaries all across the jungle and back. Think of all the people you could help." His eyes widened. "And what you could learn!"

Joseph saw himself in crisp school clothes, reading from books, exploring bustling coastal towns. His chest swelled with pride at the thought of returning to Kanweaken someday, educated and civilized.

"What do you think?" Philip asked, his face eager. Joseph opened his mouth to accept, then hesitated. "I . . . I would need to ask my parents. And the elders."

Philip nodded. "Of course, of course. But think about it, won't you? You have so much potential, Joseph. This could be the start of a bright future for you."

The next evening, Joseph sat cross-legged on the dirt floor of his family's hut. The flickering light from the cooking fire cast long shadows on the walls. His parents' faces were solemn.

"The elders have decided," his father said gently. "You will not go."

"But . . ." Joseph looked to his mother, hoping for support. There was plenty of sympathy in her eyes, but no fight. She wouldn't back his protests.

"But why?" he asked, unable to keep the desperation from his voice. "Mr. Elsea says I could get an education. I could learn so much! John, he got an education! He's not any older than I am."

Jimmy held up a hand, silencing his son. "Juty, you must understand. The world beyond our village. it is not what you think."

"Your father is right," his mother added softly. "And the elders have decided."

"We've heard stories of young people who leave," Jimmy said. "They change too much. Some never come back."

Joseph felt tears welling up but blinked them back. He was fifteen and didn't want his father to think him childish.

"And consider this," Jimmy said, his voice gentler now. "Even if you learn all they have to teach, will their people truly accept you as one of them? Or will you find yourself caught between two worlds, belonging to neither?"

His mother reached out and took his hand. "We know you're curious, Juty. We know you want to learn. But there is so much to learn here too. Give it time. Perhaps one day, when you're older, the right opportunity will come."

Joseph nodded. He knew arguing would be futile. The elders had decided, and his parents agreed. This was the way of things. But somehow, someday, he would find a way to bridge the two worlds. He would go and learn all he could, but at his core he would always be a son of Kanweaken. He would never forget where he came from.

02 | JJG

CONFLICT

The day the warriors left, the usual morning chatter in the village was replaced by hushed, solemn conversations. Joseph hurried to catch up with his older brother, Elijah, and his best friend, Marcy, walking together to the village center. Marcy's face was drawn with worry. His father, Bior, was among those leaving for battle.

The anthropologist's photos of Kanweaken life had finally reached Monrovia, and the settler government needed more men to build roads. The mining companies and the plantations needed more labor to work the land they consumed. Entire villages that had once lived and farmed on those lands were now fully dependent on the employment that the companies provided. The only other option was to pick up and move—entire villages walking and walking, hoping to find a safe place to build new huts and clear land for their farms.

The cities along the coast were growing. They needed more and more rice and cassava, and they didn't seem to think they should have to pay for it. A pair of Congo men had just left Kanweaken after counting the huts, tallying figures on a paper they gave to the Chief, telling him how much the village would owe in taxes after one year had passed.

So many young men had been taken from Palipo that the village was down to elders, overworked women, and too many hungry children. The elders of Palipo had asked Kanweaken to send warriors.

As they reached the gathering, Joseph noticed eight-year-old Mabel standing quietly beside her mother, her eyes following her father's every move. Marcy gave his sister a reassuring nod before joining the other young men.

"Off to save us from the Congos, then?" Joseph asked, trying to keep his voice light. Bior Warner smiled. "Someone's got to do it. We can't all be bookworms like you two."

Joseph and Marcy exchanged looks. Joseph felt a pang of frustration at the elders' quick blessing of war parties, while their requests to study with the Elseas were met with stern refusals. If Marcy felt any resentment, he didn't show it. He stood tall, his eyes shining with pride.

The warriors gathered in a circle, and the village elders surrounded them, offering blessings. The older women sang and danced a solemn, stately *Nyenewaleh,* encircling the warriors with outstretched hands. As younger women, and then men and children joined their voices, the song grew louder and the tone triumphant.

Even as Joseph's heart filled with admiration for the courage and skill the women were singing about, he couldn't help but wonder if there wasn't a better way to protect their people than sending their young men off to fight. But such thoughts, he knew, were best kept to himself for now. He raised his voice and added his blessings for the warriors.

Marcy joined in the prayers with fervor, his voice rising above others. Joseph watched as his friend seemed to lose himself in the spiritual energy of the moment. The Elseas had instructed them to *only* pray to their one God, but Marcy reasoned that it was better to pray with others than to pray alone, and not many in the village had wanted to keep the missionaries' God alive along with him.

In the days that followed, Joseph often found himself at Marcy's mother's hut, helping his friend look after his family and tending to tasks Bior would normally handle. Joseph read from the Bible the Elseas had entrusted him with, the only Bible in Kanweaken, while Marcy led his younger siblings in fervent prayers for their father's safe and victorious return.

As soon as the warriors had disappeared down the narrow path, the village returned to its normal rhythms. Was it quieter among the huts and in the fields, or was Joseph only imagining it?

He picked up a stick and idly scratched figures in the dirt—his own name, the magical name *Jesus* that Philip Elsea liked to say, and some other random English words. The Elseas had been gone for a year, and no one wanted to practice their language with him anymore. But if he did practice and learn it well—could it help them understand the tactics of the Congo government? Could it prevent unnecessary bloodshed?

Joseph watched with admiration as Marcy stepped into his father's role in his absence. Despite being just a few years older than Joseph, Marcy carried himself with a quiet strength that seemed beyond his years. He tended to the family's farm, looked after his younger siblings, and supported his mother with unwavering dedication.

One afternoon, as Joseph was helping Marcy repair a section of their family's hut, they heard a commotion from the village center. They rushed to see what was happening and found Ye-Mwahdoe, Marcy's mother, embroiled in a heated argument with another woman from the village.

"She stole cassava from my farm!" Marcy's mother was shouting, pointing an accusing finger at the other woman. "I caught her in the act, so I taught her a lesson!"

The woman vehemently denied the accusation, claiming that Mwahdoe had struck her without cause. "I did no such thing! The cassava I have is from my own farm!"

The villagers, perhaps swayed by the absence of Bior's strong presence, sided with the other woman. A group of men grabbed Marcy's mother and held her down as the woman she had accused beat her as punishment for causing trouble.

Joseph and Marcy were enraged when they heard about what happened to Ye-Mwahdoe. While Joseph was contemplating how to handle this matter, Marcy's reaction was swift and decisive. He marched through the village, his young face set in grim determination. He went from door to door, challenging every man, woman, and child to come out and face him.

"If you are brave enough to mistreat my mother, then be brave enough to face me!" Marcy's voice rang out, filled with a power that seemed to come from somewhere deep within him.

From sunrise to sundown, Marcy stood his ground, calling out the injustice done to his mother. He reminded them of his father's bravery, fighting for their safety even now, and shamed them for their cowardice in attacking a defenseless woman.

Joseph watched in awe as the village elders, one by one, came to Marcy to apologize. They admitted their hasty judgment and the unfairness of their actions. By the end of the day, Marcy had not only defended his mother's honor but had also earned the respect of the entire village.

That evening, as Joseph sat with Marcy's family, he saw his friend in a whole new light. Marcy had always been strong. Joseph had heard the story about how Marcy's mother, eager to induce labor, had strode in circles around the midwife's hut chanting loudly, "This baby will be strong! This baby will be a warrior! He will be great, and he will do great things!"

When the warriors finally returned, Joseph and Marcy were among the first to hear the jubilant cries. "Bior has killed their Captain!" The village erupted into a frenzy of celebration. Women ululated, men cheered, and children ran about, caught up in the infectious excitement though many didn't understand what was going on.

Everyone gathered around the central fire that night to hear what Amos, the best storyteller out of all the warriors, had to say. They learned that Bior had led the men of Kanweaken, nearby Feloken, and Palipo to ambush a group of government soldiers that was preparing to raid a small town. Though outnumbered, Bior's forces fought fiercely. When they were forced to retreat, they found themselves trapped at the edge of a wide river with no canoes to cross.

"But then," the storyteller said as his eyes gleamed with awe, "Bior called upon the ancient spirits. Before our eyes, an enormous serpent appeared! It formed a bridge for us across the water! We all got across safely and left those Congos howling. When the government forces saw this, they retreated in disarray, leaving their leader bleeding on the ground, Bior's spear through his heart." A murmur of amazement rippled through the crowd.

Jimmy squeezed Elijah's shoulder, eyes shining with pride. He said to Joseph, "You see, my son? This is why we fight. This is why we hold on to our ways. Our ancestors' power is still with us."

The celebration lasted well into the night. Drums thundered, voices raised in triumphant songs, and the palm wine-laden air was sweet with hope. Joseph found himself swept up in the jubilation, dancing with abandon in the crowd. The story of Bior's miraculous escape and victory was repeated again and again, and it grew more elaborate with each telling.

As the festivities went on, Joseph overheard snippets of conversation among the elders. They spoke of this as the moment they had been praying for, when the tide would finally turn against the government forces. "They'll leave us alone now," one elder said confidently. "They've seen the power we still possess."

But even as he joined in the celebration, a small part of Joseph couldn't help but wonder. *Was this truly the end of their struggles? Had they really defeated the government for good?*

03 | JJG

SCHOOL YEARS

News that Sherman Elsea had been born in Harper reached Kanweaken near the end of a particularly muddy rainy season. Sitting around a large fire that night, the general reaction was alarm and disbelief. If a child had really been born to Grace Elsea, what kind of child could this be? Old Man Klubo shook his head and scoffed. "Tall tales," he said.

John, who had delivered the news, refused to change his story. "It's a real baby. Not a devil baby. Ma Grace holds that baby all the time."

Jimmy held up one hand as if to slow everything down for a moment. "But do you know for sure, John, where that baby came from?"

John nodded. "Ma Grace had that baby. There are no other White ladies around, right?"

Jimmy shrugged. "It could only be hers!"

Old Man Klubo had been watching John intently as he spoke. "I'm going there to see for myself," he said.

"That's so far!" his wife, Anna, said. "How long is that going to take you? And who's going to go with you?"

Klubo glanced up at Joseph, who had been following the conversation with interest. "I'll take Joseph," he said.

A few people laughed. "Joseph? He's too busy flirting with all the girls. He's not going to want to go on some trek through the jungle to see that baby."

"I'll go!" Joseph said quickly. Four years had passed since the Elseas had left Kanweaken, but he hadn't stopped thinking about the things they had been teaching him and the schools they had told him about. He would be able to put the will of Kanweaken in writing, and the Congo government would take him seriously.

He would be able to read their laws and know when local officials were lording it over people with a heavier hand than the government allowed. Understanding the value that the Congo people attributed to the land and its resources, he would be able to demand fair compensation for his people.

"I'll go with Klubo," Joseph said again quietly. He looked around the circle and caught his father's eye. "Please think about it before you say no. Those government men will be back. If I don't go to school now, it's only a matter of time before they take me for forced labor. It would be better to go to school and get their power that way, than break my back building their roads or disappear forever into their plantations."

Jimmy lowered his head in silent agreement. He couldn't deny that what Joseph said made sense. The peace that Bior and his men's heroism had won had been short-lived. The tax men had come back, and since the village didn't have enough coin or rice to pay the bill, they had taken some of the Kanweaken's strongest young men.

The night before Joseph's departure, his mother found him sitting alone by the dying embers of the cooking fire. Without a word, she settled beside him, their shoulders barely touching.

"You should be sleeping," she said softly, poking at the coals with a stick.

Joseph shrugged. "Couldn't. Too much thinking."

They sat in comfortable silence for a while, the faint glow of the embers casting a warm light on their faces. Finally, Catherine spoke. "You know, when I was carrying you, I had the strangest dream." She paused and looked up as the moon sailed out from behind a cloud. "I saw a bird," she said slowly. "This was not a bird I recognized. It was beautiful, with feathers of every color. It flew from our village, over the trees and rivers, all the way to the sea."

Joseph turned to look at her, intrigued. "What happened then?"

"It came back," she said simply. "But when it returned, it carried seeds in its beak. Everywhere it flew, it dropped these seeds, and trees sprouted instantly."

Joseph pondered this. "What do you think it means?"

Catherine smiled, mischief in her eyes. "Well, I thought it meant you'd be a great farmer. Shows what I know."

They both muffled their laughter with their hands, mindful of the sleeping village around them.

"I think," Catherine continued, her voice growing serious, "it means you'll bring back something valuable to us. Knowledge, maybe. Hope."

Joseph nodded, feeling the weight of her expectations settle on his shoulders. "I'll do my best, Nah."

"I know you will." She reached out and squeezed his hand. "Just remember, Juty, no matter what other delicious fruits you taste out there, don't forget the flavor of our palm butter at home." A sly smile crossed her face. "And try not to lose your head over some civilized girl who doesn't know how to pound rice."

Joseph felt his cheeks grow warm. "Nah!" he protested, but he was laughing.

As they stood to return to their hut, Catherine added, "And for goodness' sake, try to send word when you can. Your father and I will be waiting to hear good things from our civilized son."

Joseph nodded. "I'll send messages with every trader who passes through."

"Good," Catherine said. "Now get some sleep. You've got a long journey ahead, and Old Man Klubo will need your eyes and ears to be extra alert."

After three days of trekking through dense jungle, Joseph and Old Man Klubo finally crested the last hill. The sight that greeted them left them both speechless. Harper sprawled before them, and it was unlike any place Joseph had ever seen. Wooden houses with tin roofs gleaming in the sun lined dirt streets in neat rows. In the distance, a large white building with a cross atop it stood out against the greenery.

But it was the endless expanse of blue beyond the town that took Joseph's breath away...the ocean! It stretched as far as the eye could see. Joseph had heard stories of the great water, but nothing had prepared him for its vastness.

Old Man Klubo also stood transfixed, his smiling face upturned. As they made their way into town, Joseph's head swiveled constantly, trying to take in every detail. Women in colorful dresses strolled by. Men in Western-style trousers and shirts hurried past. All were wearing shoes—still a rare sight in Kanweaken.

The missionary compound was a hive of activity. The sun had just risen, and children in crisp uniforms filed into a building that must be the school, their excited chatter spilling out through the open window and filling the air. Most of them were much younger than Joseph.

Philip Elsea met them at the gate, his face breaking into a wide grin. "Old Man Klubo! Joseph! Welcome to the Cape!" He ushered them into the wooden building next to the school.

Inside, they met Grace Elsea. She was standing next to a table cradling an unmistakable bundle against her shoulder. "He just fell asleep," Grace said. Old Man Klubo stepped closer, his neck craning.

As Grace pulled back the blanket to reveal little Sherman's face, Joseph watched Old Man Klubo's expression change from doubt to awe. He reached out a tentative finger to touch the baby's cheek, then broke into a toothless grin.

"It's true," he said, shaking his head in amazement. "Your God must be very powerful indeed."

Joseph, meanwhile, couldn't tear his eyes away from the school building. Through the open door he could see that the students were now sitting quietly in rows of desks. Soon he would be one of them.

Joseph's first weeks at the Elseas' mission school passed in a whirlwind of new experiences. Each day began with prayer and Bible study.

He marveled at the feel of chalk in his hand as he formed letters on a slate, the satisfying click of arithmetic beads as he solved problems, and the rhythmic sound of hammering as he helped to build an addition to the school. In the afternoons, he joined the other boys in tending the mission's garden, which was very different from his mother's farm back home with potatoes and cabbages instead of rice and cassava. He often stayed up late into the night, poring over his Bible by lamplight.

Philip Elsea was quick to praise Joseph's insatiable hunger for knowledge, but the other boys grew to resent what they saw as favoritism. When Joseph felt their critical eyes on him, he simply squared his shoulders and nodded, determined to prove himself worthy of the extra responsibility.

As time went on, Joseph found himself increasingly caught between two worlds. In class and during worship, he thrived, his voice confident and clear as he read Scripture or explained lessons to younger students. But during mealtimes and work periods, he felt the weight of his difference.

"Thinks he's a real preacher now," one boy muttered as Joseph passed.

"He thinks he's better than us, anyway," another whispered loudly.

Joseph tried to ignore the barbs, focusing instead on the joy of learning. He threw himself into every aspect of mission life, from memorizing Bible verses to learning how to mend clothes and build simple furniture. Each new skill felt like a step closer to his goal of helping Kanweaken.

One afternoon, as Joseph led a group of younger boys out to the garden, a clod of dirt struck him between his shoulder blades. He turned to see a cluster of senior students glaring at him from the other side of the potato patch. For a moment, he considered confronting them. But instead, he took a deep breath and turned back to the younger boys.

"Remember the story of David and Goliath we were just reading?" he asked. The younger boys giggled and jostled each other.

"Yes, Joseph," one of them piped up. "David defeated the giant!"

Joseph nodded, a plan forming in his mind. "That's right. Now, we have our own little challenge here. Those boys over there think they can scare us away from our work. But we're going to show them how strong we are together."

He picked up a hoe and started working on a particularly stubborn patch of weeds. "Let's see who can clear their row the fastest. And while we work, we'll sing that new hymn we learned yesterday."

The younger boys grabbed their tools and spread out along the rows, and Joseph led them in work and in chorus, his own voice strong and sure.

As they worked, Joseph noticed the older boys' scowls gradually soften and their tense shoulders drop. By the time the younger group had finished their rows, their tormentors had drifted away, leaving them to their task.

Joseph smiled to himself. This, he thought, was why he was here. Not to win popularity contests, but to learn how to become a leader. To find a way forward and share it with anyone willing to learn. Joseph soon realized that Harper, with its whitewashed church and neatly ordered missionary compound on a nearby hill, presented a convincing façade of Christian civilization. But beneath this veneer, old traditions pulsed as strong as ever. The town straddled two worlds, much like the students who filled the mission school's benches each day.

About half the pupils were local children, sent by parents who realized education was a practical necessity but who still viewed it with suspicion. In their homes, Christian hymns might mingle with the rhythm of traditional drums, and Bible verses in the mouths of the young competed with the ancient proverbs the elders still told.

The other half of the school came from villages deep in the hinterlands, like Joseph. For them, going to school was a coveted opportunity, one they had pleaded with their elders to allow. They arrived wide-eyed and determined, carrying the hopes and expectations of entire communities on their young shoulders.

This divide created an undercurrent of tension in the classroom and in the schoolyard. The local boys resented the enthusiasm of their rural counterparts. They viewed Joseph and his ilk as naïve, too eager to abandon their heritage for the White man's ways.

Joseph, for his part, struggled to understand their attitude. Didn't they see the power of this new knowledge? Couldn't they appreciate the opportunities it might bring? His earnest questions and eager participation only widened the gulf between them.

For the two years that Joseph thrived under the Elseas' tutelage, his progress was nothing short of remarkable. Now twenty-one, he had absorbed knowledge like a sponge. His natural charisma and dedication made him a favorite among the missionaries on the Elseas' compound and also among the Methodist missionaries in town.

Then came 1941. As war engulfed Europe and threatened to draw in the United States, many missionaries began to leave Africa. The Elseas, with two-year-old Sherman in tow, were no exception. In a move that spoke volumes of their trust in Joseph,

Philip left him in charge of the boys who lived at the school.

This was a responsibility Joseph took seriously, though it came with challenges his book learning hadn't prepared him for. Still a student himself, he did not command the same respect as the White missionaries. Joseph tried to maintain the routines and discipline they had established, but the other boys constantly tested boundaries and pushed back against his authority in little ways, such as a reluctance to follow instructions and conversations that fell silent when he approached.

Without the Elseas' mediating presence, old rivalries and cultural tensions bubbled to the surface. These were conflicts that went back much further than the missionaries' presence. Joseph found himself caught in an impossible position, trying to bridge a gap that seemed to widen by the day. To the local boys, his eagerness to learn all that the missionaries could teach him represented a threat to their way of life. He was a constant reminder of the changes they were being forced to accept.

What began as whispered insults soon escalated to something darker. Joseph, caught between his dreams of progress and the harsh realities of a world not ready to change, was about to learn a painful lesson about the cost of ambition.

The sun hung low in the sky as Joseph left the schoolhouse that evening. His mind was so busy running through the multiplication tables he was trying to memorize, he barely noticed the group of boys trailing behind him until they called out.

"Hey, smart boy! We've got a question for you."

Joseph turned, his heart sinking as he saw the familiar faces of his tormentors. They formed a loose circle around him, their eyes glinting with malice.

"What are you still doing here?" one sneered. "If you're so clever, how come you don't know we don't want you here?"

Joseph's eyes darted from face to face, searching for a way out. He opened his mouth to speak, but before he could utter a word, a fist connected with his jaw.

Pain exploded across his face. Instinct took over. Joseph's arm shot out, his knuckles finding flesh and bone. A sickening crunch. The boy crumpled to the ground. Silence fell. Then chaos erupted.

The other boys scattered, their shouts echoing as they ran down the hill to the village. Joseph froze, staring at the unconscious form at his feet. Blood roared in his ears.

He stood over the unconscious boy until men from the village arrived, wafting herbs and praying to the spirits, and they carried him away.

Night fell, and Joseph went to his room. A soft knock at his door some hours later woke him from a troubled sleep. An older man from the village stood there, his eyes darting nervously.

"You must leave," he whispered. "I overheard the elders. They plan to . . . It's not safe for you here anymore."

Joseph's world tilted. Leave? How could he abandon his dreams of education? How could he go home bringing so little? Yet as the man's words sank in, fear took hold. Joseph nodded, his throat too tight for words.

He packed up his school clothes and books, took a torch, and slipped out into the night soon after the man left. The forest loomed before him, dark and forbidding. Joseph took a deep breath and kept walking.

He walked for hours, the sounds of the night forest setting his nerves on edge. When he reached the river, the water gleamed black in the moonlight. Joseph hesitated, then waded in. The current tugged at his legs, threatening to sweep him away.

Somehow, he made it across. As dawn broke, Joseph found himself in unfamiliar territory. His stomach gnawed with hunger. His clothes, still damp from the river crossing, clung uncomfortably to his skin.

Exhaustion finally overtook him. Joseph sank to the forest floor, his back against a massive tree trunk. As he huddled there, cold and alone, regret washed over him. He thought of Kanweaken, of his family, of the simple life he had left behind. For the first time, Joseph wondered if he had made a terrible mistake.

In response to the hundreds of questions that his family and friends asked when he returned home, Joseph shared what he could about his experiences at the mission compound. He mainly focused on what he had learned and how he hoped to use that knowledge, saying little about the violent confrontation that had forced his departure.

It surprised him how easy it was to fall back into the daily rhythm of work, socializing, and relaxation, almost as if he had never left. His muscles had forgotten nothing. He helped clear land for his sisters' farms, now that they were grown and married, and then he helped plant and harvest those farms. The following year, the cycle repeated. He began gathering the village children in the early mornings as the Elseas had done, teaching them to practice basic English phrases before they went off to the farms with their mothers.

For the children who wanted to spend more time learning, he collected flat pieces of smooth stone from the creek, carefully selecting those with light, even surfaces. Soft, white clay found in certain layers of soil became a substitute for chalk, perfect for practicing letters and numbers. The children delighted in the way the clay easily washed off with a splash of water.

As the months passed, Joseph's concern for Kanweaken's future grew. News trickled in from travelers about the rapid changes sweeping across Liberia. Villages to the north had been displaced by expanding mining operations. Each year, more young men from Kanweaken were taken to work on rubber plantations or in government construction projects, and their families wondered if they would ever make it back.

One evening, as Joseph sat with his family around the cooking fire, his father spoke of the latest rumors. "They say the government men are coming again soon," he said, his voice low. "The hut taxes are higher than ever."

Joseph's mother shook her head. "How can we pay? The harvest was poor this year, and we barely have enough to feed ourselves."

Joseph looked at his younger siblings. There was Philip, now a lanky teenager, and his youngest sisters, still children but growing quickly. He wondered what kind of future they would face if things continued as they were.

"We need to be prepared," Joseph said, his voice firm. "Education is key. If our people can read and write, they'll be better equipped to deal with the government, to understand their rights."

"You could be right, son. But even if school is a good thing, will it be enough?"

Joseph spent many nights pondering this question. He knew the rudimentary lessons he was providing were just a beginning. Kanweaken needed more. They needed a proper school with trained teachers and real books and supplies. But where would all these come from?

One day, as Joseph was teaching under the shade of a large tree, the village suddenly went silent. He looked up to see that a group of government officials had arrived, accompanied by armed soldiers. Their crisp uniforms and stern faces contrasted sharply with the simple attire of the villagers. The tax collectors, brandishing papers and shouting demands, began moving from hut to hut. Joseph's students scattered, fear evident in their wide eyes. He quickly made his way to Klubo's hut, where he knew the government men were headed.

"You must pay your taxes!" one official shouted, his face with anger. "It is your duty to the government!"

An elder tried to speak. "But sir, we have so little. The harvest was poor this year, and we—"

A soldier roughly shoved the old man, cutting off his words. Joseph felt a surge of anger and stepped forward. "Stop!" he called out in clear English, surprising the officials. "You can't treat our people this way. They don't have money to spare, and they don't even know what these taxes are for. How can you demand payment when they see no benefit?"

The lead official turned to Joseph, eyes narrowing. "And who do you think you are to question government business?" he sneered.

Joseph stood his ground. "I am a son of Kanweaken, an educated man, and these are my people. They deserve to understand what they're paying for."

There was silence for a moment. Then, without warning, the butt of a rifle swung through the air. Pain exploded across Joseph's face as it connected with his mouth. He tasted blood and felt the sickening shift inside his mouth of broken teeth giving way.

"That'll teach you not to talk back," the soldier growled.

Joseph staggered, spitting blood. The villagers cried out in shock and anger. For a heartbeat, it seemed they might retaliate, and he couldn't let that happen. The government men had guns, while the villagers didn't.

Joseph, despite the pain, raised his hands. "No!" he managed to say through the pain. "We'll fight them another way."

The officials and soldiers backed away. One of them handed Klubo an envelope—the tax bill—before they left.

"If they want to take taxes from us, then we must demand the benefits we're owed. Schools, roads, clinics. That's what they're supposed to provide," Joseph told the elders a few nights later. "We need to ensure that all our children have the opportunity to learn, to understand the world beyond our village. Only then can we hope to preserve our way of life." He added quietly, "It sounds strange, but we need to change some small things so that what's most important—our family bonds, our ability to care for our children and keep our village safe—can stay the same."

Joseph's heart swelled when he saw his father nodding along with what he was saying, and his voice grew stronger, despite the pain. "We need to learn how their system works so we can change it." He brought his hand to his tender jaw and winced. "I know it won't be easy, and it won't happen quickly. But we must try."

From that day forward, Joseph dedicated himself not just to teaching the children of Kanweaken, but to educating everyone in the village who was open to learning. He told them everything he had learned in Harper about their rights and the workings of the government. "It's supposed to be a government for everybody," he often said. "That means it's supposed to be for us too." He knew it would be a long struggle, but he was determined to see it through. The future of Kanweaken depended on it.

04 | JG

BACK IN KANWEAKEN

Joseph was knee-deep in the cassava patch when shouts erupted from the edge of the village. He straightened, wiping sweat from his brow, and squinted toward the commotion. A crowd was gathering, their excited voices carrying across the fields.

"Teacher Joe! Teacher Joe!" A breathless child skidded to a stop beside him. "There's a White lady asking for you! She came right out of the jungle!"

Joseph's eyebrows shot up. A White lady? Here? This would be the first White woman in Kanweaken since Grace Elsea left for Cape Palmas just over ten years ago. Almost all of the missionaries in the region had gone back to the United States when their country entered World War II three years ago. So who could this be?

Curiosity piqued, he hurried toward the commotion. As he approached, the crowd parted, revealing a sight that nearly made him laugh out loud. There, looking like she'd wrestled with every vine in the forest, stood a determined-looking woman who appeared quite a bit older than most of the missionary women he had met at Cape Palmas. Her safari outfit was rumpled and sweat-stained, leaves and twigs clinging to her as if the jungle was reluctant to let her go.

"Joseph?" she called out, her voice carrying notes of hope and exhaustion.

"That's me!" He stepped forward. "And you are . . . ?"

"Lois Shelton," she said. "I've trekked for a whole day to find you." Her eyes met his briefly, and then she looked around eagerly at the village.

"You walked? No hammock? No guides? Where did you come from?"

Lois shook her head. "It was foolish of me, I know, and it shouldn't have taken that long. I just came from Feloken."

Joseph's friendly grin widened. He liked her already. "And what brings a lady like yourself thrashing through the jungle to our village? Just to find me?"

Lois' eyes sparkled. She lowered her voice, as if afraid the wrong person might hear, and said, "Oh, just a little project. Nothing much. I'm planning to start a school between here and Feloken, and the Elseas told me you were the one to ask for help."

Joseph felt a jolt of excitement. "I might be. Depends on whether you're planning to teach anything useful or just how to sing hymns and look pretty on Sunday."

Lois laughed out loud. "Oh, we'll sing hymns all right. But we'll also teach reading, writing, arithmetic, and anything else these children need."

Still keeping his tone light, Joseph said, "Well, Miss Shelton, I would be happy to help. We will need to check with the elders."

As Joseph led Lois toward the elders' meeting place, his mind raced with the possibilities. A school that would serve both Kanweaken and Feloken . . . maybe there really had been a God listening to his prayers.

Then his thoughts turned to Mabel, daughter of the warrior Bior Warner whose brave heroism had won the villages a brief period of peace before war broke out across Europe and the foreigners became hungrier than ever for the hinterland's minerals and rubber. Mabel had been one of Joseph's most enthusiastic students before her father died and she was sent away at ten years old. He had heard that she had grown up to be a strong and graceful young woman, and he wondered what she would remember of him. Marcy had left Kanweaken in answer to a nearby village's request for a preacher shortly before Joseph returned from the Elsea's school in Cape Palmas.

Sometime after Bior Warner's death, his family became indebted to another family in Feloken, and young Mabel was sent to live with that family. Her betrothal to one of their sons was intended to settle the debt, and she went to work on her future mother-in-law's farm while waiting for the wedding to take place.

Then the man she was supposed to marry died, and it was agreed that Mabel would marry one of his brothers instead. Years had gone by, though, and Mabel was still unmarried, still working on her future mother-in-law's fields.

Joseph's heart ached thinking of the bright, determined girl he had taught to sing the alphabet before she was sent away—years ago, before he had followed the Elseas to the coast. He remembered how quickly she grasped the language. Now, instead of pursuing her education or starting her own family as most young women did at her age, she spent her days trapped in an in-between life.

When Mabel was sent away, her mother cleared a new patch of farmland close to the farm where Mabel worked, and built a small hut so she could stay there for days at a time to be closer to her daughter. This farm was a long walk from Kanweaken and not as protected as the areas the other women farmed.

Whenever Mabel went to the river for chores, she could see her mother's farm on the other side. Eventually she acquired a canoe so she was able to cross the river and share meals with her mother. This she did every chance she got.

"Miss Shelton," Joseph said, slowing his pace, "this school you're proposing . . . where exactly are you planning to build it?"

"We've found a suitable location about halfway between Kanweaken and Feloken. It's on a hill, which should keep it dry during the rainy season."

"Which side of the river?" Joseph asked.

"The Feloken side."

Joseph nodded. "That could work well." He paused, then said, "There's a young girl in Feloken I used to teach. She's incredibly bright, but circumstances have forced her to stop her education. Do you think there might be a place for her in your school?"

Lois' eyes softened. "Of course, Joseph. Our doors will be open to any child eager to learn. Tell me about her."

As they continued walking, Joseph shared Mabel's story. He spoke of her quick mind, her determination, and only hinted at the unfairness of her situation.

"Joseph," Lois said, "I can see why the Elseas spoke so highly of you. Your passion for education, your concern for your students . . . this is exactly why I want you to teach in my school."

Joseph was still unmarried at twenty-five, something almost unheard of. His older brother, Elijah, had already started a family, and Joseph enjoyed being a "favorite uncle" to his little niece and nephew. It wasn't that he didn't dream of home life with a wife and children. But he wanted to be free to seize upon any opportunity that might come up to help his community get on better footing with the encroaching Western world, and he didn't want any responsibilities at home to get in the way. He had been starting to wonder lately if forgoing family life had been the right decision. But now, with the possibility of this new school and helping students like Mabel, he knew he was on the right path.

Night fell as they approached the elders' meeting place, and campfires flared up outside the huts. Joseph squared his shoulders. He knew convincing the elders wouldn't be easy, but he was determined to make this work for Kanweaken, for Mabel, and for all the children who deserved a chance to create a better future. They deserved to learn what was going on and find ways to defend their home and their interests beyond using guns or spears.

The air in the large meeting hut was thick with the sweet smell of palm wine, a libation that was traditionally present at ceremonial and social gatherings. Joseph stood beside Lois, facing the semicircle of the weathered faces of the men who had watched over him and guided decisions for him all his life. He took a deep breath, acutely aware of the weight of his words.

"Honored elders," Joseph began in Grebo, his voice steady, "Miss Shelton proposes to build a school that will serve both Kanweaken and Feloken. She asks for my help in teaching, and for some of our most promising children to attend."

A murmur rippled through the gathering. Elder Klubo, his face etched with skepticism, spoke first.

"And who will work the farms if our children are at this school? Who will learn the ways of our ancestors?"

Joseph nodded. "I understand your fears. We've seen too many of our young men lured away to the mines and plantations by promises of work, only to be trapped in harsh conditions they can't escape." He paused to let what he said next sink in. "But this school is going to be different. It's not about turning our backs on our traditions. We need to arm our children with knowledge to protect our way of life."

Another elder leaned forward. "How can we be sure? So many have left, thinking they would become great men in the world of the foreigners. Instead, they become slaves to companies and governments. These governments have taken so much from us already and have not fulfilled even one of their promises. They said they would build a school too."

Joseph turned to Lois and translated these concerns.

"Please tell them," she said to Joseph, "that I've met with the new president of Liberia, President Tubman, and he has a vision for the country that's going to change everything. He speaks of a unified Liberia, one where the people of the hinterland are treated with respect and included at the table."

Joseph felt his jaw drop in surprise. "You . . . met with the most powerful man in the country?"

Lois nodded enthusiastically. "I did. I was stuck in Monrovia for eleven weeks, waiting for transportation to Cape Palmas. In desperation, I went to see President Tubman. He's quite democratic, you know. Anyone willing to wait their turn can see him." As Joseph translated, he saw the elders' eyes widen with interest.

"President Tubman asked me about our school," Lois continued. "When I explained the situation, he personally helped arrange my travel here, despite the difficulties of the war. He gave me a letter that secured my place on a plane." [1]

The mention of such a powerful connection clearly carried weight with the elders. Joseph could see them exchanging thoughtful glances.

Lois pressed on. "I'm not here to take children away from their culture. I want to give them tools to navigate both worlds. They'll learn to read, write, and calculate, yes, but they'll also learn about their rights, about the laws that govern this land. With President

---

[1] Lois Shelton describes this incident on pages 55–56 in her autobiographical book *Tell Me*, published in 1949.

Tubman's new vision, education will be key to ensuring your people have a voice in Liberia's future."

Joseph added, his voice passionate, "Imagine our children able to read contracts, to understand the laws that affect our lives. They won't be easy to trick or exploit! They'll be decision-makers, with allies in powerful places. I will ensure our children learn what they need without forgetting who they are."

A long silence followed. Finally, one of the elders spoke. "We have seen the world changing around us. Perhaps . . . perhaps it is time we changed, too, but on our own terms."

Old Man Klubo nodded thoughtfully.

The decision of the elders was delivered the next day. Joseph and four students of his choosing would go with Lois to help her establish the school.

05 | JJG

A FAMILY MAN

J oseph wiped sweat from his brow as he made his way along the dusty paths, approaching the field where he knew he would find Mabel harvesting rice. He'd made a habit of visiting when he could, bringing books and offering her a chance to practice English as he worked alongside her.

There was Mabel's slender form among the rows. She looked up, a smile brightening her tired face as she recognized him.

"Teacher Joe," she called out, straightening up. "I didn't expect to see you today."

Joseph was about to respond when he heard quick footsteps behind him. He turned to see Lois Shelton approaching, her expression curious.

"Miss Shelton," Joseph said, surprised. "I didn't realize you'd followed me."

Lois smiled apologetically. "I hope you don't mind, Joseph. I was intrigued when I saw you heading this way with that hymnal."

Joseph introduced the two women, watching as Lois took in Mabel's worn dress and calloused hands. Despite her obvious exhaustion, Mabel carried herself with quiet dignity.

"Joseph tells me you're quite the eager student," Lois said warmly.

Mabel's eyes lit up. "Teacher Joe has been so kind, bringing me books and teaching me when he can."

As Joseph and Mabel fell into an impromptu lesson, Lois observed them silently. Joseph spelled and pronounced words, and Mabel repeated them as they worked.

Later, as they walked back to the school, Lois turned to Joseph. "That young woman, Mabel . . . she's the one you were telling me about back in Kanweaken. It's a shame she can't attend our school regularly." Joseph nodded, his expression somber. "It is. But her situation . . . it's complicated."

Lois raised an eyebrow, inviting him to elaborate, but Joseph merely shook his head. "It's not my story to tell, Miss Shelton. But yes, it is a shame."

Weeks passed, and Lois again accompanied Joseph on one of his visits to Mabel. Each time, she saw more of the young woman's potential—and more of the connection between her and Joseph. Mabel sat bent over the book of hymns Joseph had brought her, reading the words out loud.

Lois stepped closer to Joseph. "She's making remarkable progress, considering how little time she has to study." she whispered.

Joseph nodded, pride evident in his eyes. "She's brilliant, Miss Shelton. If only . . ."He trailed off, but Lois pressed gently. "If only what, Joseph?"

Joseph sighed, glancing at Mabel to ensure she was engrossed in her reading. "If only she were free to pursue her education fully. To make her own choices."

Lois' brow furrowed. "What do you mean, 'free'? Surely her family . . ."

Just then Mabel closed the book and held it out to Joseph. "*En whemonoh!*" she said in Grebo ("I've finished!"). Then she added in English, "And it is well with my soul."

Walking back to the mission compound that night, Lois and Joseph sang together, "It is well . . . it is well . . . with my soul!"

Fig. 1 - Young Mabel Warner

After a pause, Lois asked again, "Joseph, what did you mean about Mabel's freedom? She's not married ?"

"It's not that simple," Joseph said, his voice low. "She's betrothed."

Lois gave him a quizzical look.

"It's more that her family owes a debt, and she's the payment."

Lois didn't try to hide her shock. "Betrothed? But she's a grown woman! And to whom?"

"That's the thing..." Joseph said, his frustration creeping into his voice. "The man she was chosen to marry has died, or the wedding would have happened years ago. Now she's not even appointed to a specific person. Just . . . one of the brothers in the family her family is indebted to. All of whom already have multiple wives."

Lois shook her head. "I shouldn't say this, but I think that's . . . barbaric. Surely there's something to be done."

Joseph shrugged helplessly. "These are old traditions, Miss Shelton, not easily changed."

Lois sat down at her desk early one morning a few days later and realized she still had forty-five minutes before the students would begin to arrive. She took out the handwritten manuscript she had been working on—a book-length answer to all the questions people back home asked her about her life in Africa.

She wrote:

Marriage is not usually the sequel to a love affair. Frequently, a girl is promised only to a family, and the family head decides whose wife she shall be. Sometimes the girl lives in the head mother's house under her supervision so she will learn the likes and dislikes of her future husband's family. She becomes accustomed to the idea and seldom objects to marrying the one appointed to her.

Theoretically, she may refuse . . .[2]

Lois stopped writing and rolled her pen between her fingers. Could a girl like Mabel really refuse?

Just then, the sound of the door creaking open and clicking shut caused her to look up. Joseph entered, looking apologetic. "I'm sorry to disturb your writing, Miss Shelton. I just wanted to return this book I loaned to Mabel."

Lois waved away his apology and gestured for him to sit. "I was just thinking about Mabel," she said, "And you." She gave him an encouraging smile, which he returned. She'd seen the way Joseph looked at Mabel, the gentle care in his interactions with her. It was more than just a teacher's concern for a student.

"She can refuse the betrothal, can't she? How can one girl be responsible for her whole family's debt? And she's waited for so long."

Joseph allowed the room to go silent after Lois' voice trailed off.

---

[2] Shelton, *Tell Me*, x.

"You care for her," Lois finally said. It wasn't a question.

"I do," Joseph said firmly. "But what does it matter as long as she's bound by this arrangement?"

Lois felt something stir within her—a sense of injustice, yes, but also a growing resolve. "Joseph," she said, "I may be about to do something foolish. But too many opportunities have gone by where I could have done some good and didn't. Mabel is not the kind of girl to try to save herself, and she shouldn't have to."

Joseph's eyes widened. "Miss Shelton, you can't possibly mean . . ."

Lois held up a hand. "I'm not making any promises, but let me think about this. Perhaps there's a way we can give Mabel a chance at a different future."

As Joseph left her office, hope warring with disbelief on his face, Lois turned back to her writing pad. She murmured, "I know Lord, I probably shouldn't meddle. I'm old enough to know better."

The next time Lois found Mabel alone, she was working in a field near the school.

"Mabel," she called softly.

The young woman looked up and smiled. "Miss Shelton! Is everything all right?"

Lois took a deep breath. "Mabel, I want to talk to you about something important. Your situation . . . your betrothal."

Mabel's smile faded, replaced by a guarded expression.

"I've been thinking," Lois began carefully. "You work hard, and you're good-hearted. I can tell. You're also such a good student. Joseph talks so often about how bright you are. You shouldn't be held back by this arrangement. I . . . I'm prepared to pay your family's debt to free you from this betrothal."

Mabel's eyes widened in shock. To Lois' surprise, she shook her head vigorously. "Miss Shelton, I . . . I don't know what to say. That's incredibly generous, but . . ." Mabel trailed off, looking conflicted.

"But what, Mabel?" Lois prompted gently.

Mabel's voice was barely above a whisper when she replied. "What kind of future would that leave me? A woman who broke off a betrothal?"

Lois felt her heart sink. "But surely, with education and with the chance to choose your own path . . ."

Mabel shook her head again. "It's not just about me. It's about my family's honor, and about keeping our word. If I were to break this arrangement, it would bring shame not just on me, but on my entire family. No one would want to marry me after that."

Lois felt a wave of frustration. "But, Mabel, you're so bright. You have so much potential. Surely there must be a way . . ."

"I appreciate your offer, truly," Mabel said, her eyes glistening with unshed tears. "But this is the world I live in. I can't just abandon my responsibilities, no matter how much I might want to."

Joseph was grading math quizzes when Lois burst into the classroom, her face flushed.

"Joseph, I've done something . . . well, I'm not sure if it was foolish or brave," she said, sinking into a nearby chair. "Anyway, I've done it."

Joseph set down his pen, giving Lois his full attention.

Lois took a deep breath. "I spoke to Mabel. I offered to pay her family's debt to free her from the betrothal."

Joseph's heart leapt, then immediately sank as he took in the conflicted expression on Lois' face. "What did she say?" It wasn't completely unheard of for girls to break off betrothals. Still scandalous, but not completely unthinkable.

"She refused," Lois said, shaking her head. "They tell you there are things money can't buy ."

Joseph had known it wouldn't be simple, but hearing about Mabel's refusal still stung. He considered going and having a conversation of his own with Mabel.

Then he thought about how so many of the missionaries—the ones who stayed, anyway—were not married. More to the point, it was the unmarried women who tended to stay. There was one missionary man he'd heard of at Cape Palmas who had no officially wedded wife, but at the same time, he seemed to have at least a few informal wives in every village. The husband-and-wife teams he saw were constantly torn between the work they wanted to do in the world and their obligations at home. Joseph knew that he had a lot of work to do, and he didn't want to be distracted by matters at home.

Mabel, though—she saw things the way he did, and she believed in the vision he had secretly shared with her for their people. He had a feeling that he could accomplish a lot more with her by his side. He would go to her. They would accept Lois' offer, and they would pay back every cent as soon as they could.

"I'm going to be very direct with you, Joseph." Lois interrupted his thoughts. "I'm sorry to be a busybody, but maybe if you speak to her and make an offer of your own . . ."

Joseph stood up, his heart pounding. He could feel the grin stretching across his face. "I will go and talk with Mabel. I think we can find a way."

Building, planting, studying, teaching. Mending and washing uniforms, and mending them again. Mabel and Joseph were busy! Their days began before sunrise and often stretched late into the night.

Joseph constantly moved between roles - teacher, student, construction laborer, farm hand, and now husband. He led classes in English and mathematics, poring over lesson plans late into the night to ensure he was providing the best education possible for his eager pupils.

Mabel threw herself into her new life with enthusiasm. Her natural warmth and nurturing spirit made her a favorite in the community, especially among the younger students, many of whom were away from home for the first time. She could often be found comforting a homesick child or patiently helping a struggling student with their lessons.

Beyond academics, the couple took on numerous practical tasks to keep the school running smoothly. Joseph repaired desks and mended leaky roofs, while Mabel tended to the school's large garden, supplementing their meals with fresh vegetables. The donut-like pastries (*frialor*) they fried together were talked about in all the surrounding villages, and people often joked that these special treats were the real reason children came to the school from miles around.

Lois had paid Mabel's family's debt, and Joseph was working to pay her back. As soon as Mabel was free, she and Joseph had a traditional wedding in Kanweaken. It had been over ten years since Mabel had left, and her return was celebrated with gusto. The feasting and dancing went on for days. Then, as soon as the dust settled, the newlyweds went back to Lois' school outside Feloken.

Lois was eager for the couple to have a Christian wedding now that they were traditionally married. Mabel agreed with the idea, and Joseph was compliant. But that would have to wait until a preacher came through again. That was a credential Lois didn't have. There were a few Grebo men who had been educated at the mission schools and ordained as preachers, but they were scattered across the region. Mabel's brother

Marcy, being one of them. Lois was the only American missionary who had been able to return to Liberia since the war in Europe broke out.

The rainy season started early that year. Joseph got up from his desk to close the door against the gusty rain and noticed a figure stumbling up the muddy path. Squinting against the drizzle, his heart skipped a beat when he recognized the approaching woman. "Meissen?" he whispered, hardly believing his eyes.

Before he could move, Mabel rushed past him, calling out to the newcomer. Joseph watched as his wife reached Meissen just as the girl swayed dangerously. He hurried to help, taking in Meissen's gaunt face and fever-bright eyes. Meissen was one of the students who lived with Mabel and Joseph. This arrangement was made by the missionaries due to the overfilling of students. Every married couple on the mission ground was assigned few students to care for.

As they guided her inside, Joseph's mind raced. Meissen was a girl Joseph had often enjoyed spending time with, and family members had started to murmur about the possibility of a wedding on the horizon—though at that time Joseph felt it would be better to stay single. Meissen had been so vibrant and healthy when he had said goodbye to her in Kanweaken, just two short months ago. What could have brought her here in such a state?

Joseph stood back as Mabel tended to Meissen in her parlor. His chest tightened as Mabel assessed Meissen's health and peeled her soaked clothing away from her too-thin body.

"We were children together in Kanweaken," Mabel was explaining softly to Lois, "before I was sent to Feloken. I haven't seen her since I was ten."

Meissen's eyes fluttered open, focusing on Mabel for a brief second before looking past her. "They said you were here," she managed, her voice barely above a whisper, "Said you had a new life. I didn't know where else to go."

Joseph felt a pang of guilt. He had left Kanweaken to pursue his education, leaving behind many, including Meissen. Had his actions contributed to her current state?

As the days passed and Meissen regained her strength, Joseph found himself drawn to her bedside, sharing stories of Kanweaken and catching up on years of missed history. He marveled at Mabel's unwavering dedication to nursing Meissen back to health, showing no hint of jealousy or resentment.

One evening, as Joseph sat with Meissen on the schoolhouse's verandah, she turned to him with troubled eyes. "Joseph," she began hesitantly, "there's something I need to tell you."

His heart raced. "What is it, Meissen?"

She took a deep breath. "I'm . . . I'm pregnant, Joseph, and it's yours."

Joseph's mind reeled. The implications of this revelation threatened everything he had built with Mabel—his position at the school and his future plans. Mabel was pregnant too.

"We should tell Mabel," Meissen said, her tone anxious.

Joseph nodded, his thoughts in turmoil. "We will," he replied, trying to sound reassuring despite his own fears. "But let's wait until you're stronger. There's no need to burden her now. She also is pregnant."

The afternoon sun hung low in the sky, casting long shadows across the schoolyard as Mabel finished sweeping the classroom floor. She paused, leaning on her broom, one hand resting on the slight swell of her belly. A shout from outside caught her attention.

"Sister! Little sister!"

Mabel's eyes widened. She knew that voice. Dropping the broom, she hurried to the doorway just in time to see a familiar figure striding up the path, arms outstretched.

"Marcy!" she cried, rushing to meet him. Her brother swept her into a hug, then held her at arm's length, his eyes twinkling. "Look at you! Married and with child. I hardly recognize my little sister anymore."

Mabel laughed, swatting his arm playfully. "Oh, stop it. You haven't been gone that long."

As they walked toward the school building, Marcy's eyes darted around, taking in the neatly tended garden, the rows of desks visible through open windows, and the small cluster of white wooden buildings that made up the mission compound. The one mud hut in the center of the compound was where Lois lived. She had built it herself, saying that the local people knew better than anyone how to build for their climate, and the wooden buildings everyone else thought were so prestigious needed too much upkeep in this humid climate.

"So this is where you've been hiding, eh? Quite a change from Ma's farm."

Joseph watched the interaction as he approached, and he noted with pleasure how similar the smiles of Mabel and her brother were. It wasn't just that their mannerisms were alike because they were siblings. Mabel had a way of mirroring people that brought out their best qualities.

Marcy hurried to meet Joseph, and the two men embraced, slapping each other on the back. "Brother! It's good to see you," Joseph said warmly.

As the sun dipped below the horizon, they gathered around a small fire outside, joined by Lois and a few of the older students. Marcy regaled them with tales of his travels as a roaming preacher.

"You wouldn't believe the things I've seen." he said, his eyes gleaming in the firelight. "Just last month, I was in a village so deep in the hinterland none of you have even heard of it yet."

He leaned forward, his voice dropping dramatically. "Something was going around in that village, making people sick, children and elders especially. Children were falling sick left and right. The people were desperate, ready to try anything."

"The devil," Mabel whispered. Lois nodded.

"I gathered a bunch of people together and showed them how to pray the Christian way." He closed his eyes and clasped his hands. "We prayed like I had never prayed before. And then, just as we said 'Amen', a woman came running into the clearing. Her little girl, who'd been at death's door that morning, was sitting up, asking for food!"

Gasps and murmurs rippled through the group.

"The elders decided then and there they wanted to build a church."

Lois clasped her hands together, her eyes shining. "Brother Marcy, what a wonderful story. The Lord truly works in mysterious ways."

Joseph nodded, but Mabel noticed a slight furrow in his brow. She knew he sometimes struggled with the idea that faith alone could solve all problems.

As the students drifted off to their different assignments, Lois turned to Marcy with a hopeful expression. "Marcy, since you're here . . . well, we've been hoping to have Joseph and Mabel married in a proper Christian ceremony. Would you be willing to officiate?"

Marcy's face lit up. "It would be my honor! What do you say, little sister? Ready to walk down the Lord's aisle?"

Mabel smiled, glancing at Joseph. "I think that would be lovely. Don't you, Joe?"

Joseph nodded, squeezing Mabel's hand. "Of course. It would mean a lot to have you perform the ceremony, Marcy." He smiled to cover the anxiousness he felt about the difficult conversations ahead.

As it turned out, Joseph was relieved of the burden of starting those difficult conversations. It was Old Man Juwillie, Meissen's father, who broke the news to everyone at the mission compound. Two days before Joseph's wedding to Mabel, as Joseph hefted a crate of books towards the schoolhouse, he turned and saw Old Man Juwillie striding through the compound's main gate.

Joseph had always liked the man. A member of the tribal council, he upheld the traditional ways of life that shaped the community. No decision was made, no action taken without his counsel. He had built his own wooden house outside the school grounds before any other such houses were built in Kanweaken.

Seeing the hard glint in Juwillie's eyes as he marched toward the schoolhouse, filled with silently studying children, Joseph felt a chill. He had no doubt about the reason Meissen's father had come.

The news of Joseph and Mabel's impending Christian wedding must have reached him; and with it, the realization that his own daughter, Meissen, was being left behind.

Joseph set down the crate, his mind racing. He had hoped to have more time, to find a way to honor his responsibilities to both Mabel and Meissen without upending everything he'd worked for. But Juwillie's presence made it clear - time had run out.

Straightening his shoulders, Joseph moved to intercept Old Man Juwillie before he could reach Lois. Perhaps there was still a chance to manage this quietly. But as Juwillie's eyes locked on him, blazing with righteous anger, Joseph knew that hope was futile. The reckoning he'd feared had arrived, and with it, the end of the simple future he'd dared to imagine.

The elder's voice cut through the air. "Joseph Geleplay! How dare you plan this farce of a wedding?"

Heads turned across the compound. Joseph winced, acutely aware of the curious stares from students and staff alike. "Old Man Juwillie," he began, keeping his voice low, "perhaps we could discuss this privately..."

"Discuss?" Juwillie scoffed. "There's nothing to discuss. You have a responsibility to my daughter, to the child she carries. Your child."

The words hung in the air, heavy and damning. From the corner of his eye, Joseph saw Mabel freeze, her eyes wide.

Lois and Marcy hurried over.

Lois said, "Mr. Juwillie, what's going on here?"

"Miss Shelton, you can't allow this wedding. Meissen must be Joseph's first wife. Not Mabel.

"Old Man Juwillie," Marcy said, his voice low, "perhaps we should discuss this privately, away from curious ears."

"This doesn't concern you, son," Juwillie growled.

"It concerns my sister," Marcy replied, "and the honor of our family."

Lois nodded and motioned for everyone to follow her into a classroom, where she closed the door.

As they walked by Mabel, Joseph tried to give her a reassuring look. The hurt and confusion he saw in her eyes made his chest ache.

Lois stared at Joseph, waiting for his explanation.

"Both women carry my child," he said quietly. "I have a responsibility to both of them."

At the same time, Juwillie was saying, "Joseph will marry Meissen in a proper Christian wedding. He is the father of her child, so it's the only right thing to do."

Marcy raised his hand for silence, then said, "Joseph has already married my sister Mabel according to our traditions. He's also willing to marry Meissen the same way. Isn't that the most honorable path?"

Joseph nodded, grateful for Marcy's support. "I will marry Mabel in the church as we have planned. She is the only woman I will marry in the church. Meissen will be my second wife, and I will pay a dowry for her."

"No!" Juwillie exploded. "I didn't raise my daughter to be treated like this! She will be your first wife, and she will be a civilized wife!"

The room fell silent. Joseph's mind raced, searching for a solution that could satisfy everyone. But as he looked between Juwillie's righteous anger and Lois' disappointment, and as he thought of Mabel's hurt, he realized there might not be one.

Lois sighed, her disappointment evident. "Then I'm afraid there can be no church wedding, Joseph. And you can't continue living on the mission grounds if you're practicing polygamy."

Juwillie bristled, but Marcy interrupted before he could speak. "Joseph is doing the right thing by both women according to our ways. Shouldn't that count for something?"

In the end, Joseph agreed to build a house off the mission grounds for his growing family. He would marry Meissen according to Grebo tradition, just as he had married Mabel. There would be no church wedding, but he would honor his commitments to both women.

As they left the school building, Marcy put a hand on Joseph's shoulder. "I'll speak with the elders," he said quietly. "They'll understand you're doing the honorable thing for both women and their children."

Not willing to give up his case, Juwillie set out on a determined journey to seek justice as he saw it. His first stop was Tiehnpo, the village of the Paramount Chief. However, unbeknownst to Juwillie, Marcy had anticipated his moves and was one step ahead.

When Juwillie arrived to plead his case before the Paramount Chief, he found Marcy already there, ready to present Joseph and Mabel's side of the story. As Juwillie demanded that Joseph be forced to marry Meissen in the church, Marcy calmly explained that Joseph was already traditionally married to Mabel and had honorably offered to marry Meissen in the same way.

The Paramount Chief, hearing both sides and impressed by Marcy's mature handling of the situation, threw the case out. But Juwillie was not deterred.

Over the following weeks, Juwillie took his case to every magistrate he could find in the region. And at every turn, Marcy was there, having traveled ahead or alongside, ready to defend his sister Mabel's honor. He tirelessly repeated the facts: Joseph had acted honorably toward both women according to their traditions.

Magistrate after magistrate heard the case, and each time, with Marcy's unwavering advocacy, they came to the same conclusion: Joseph's actions were just and in line with their customs. Juwillie's demands for a church wedding for Meissen were repeatedly denied.

Marcy's persistence and eloquence in defending Joseph and Mabel's cause became well known throughout the region. His actions not only protected his sister's honor but also reinforced the community's respect for Joseph's integrity.

Joseph stepped back and admired the wooden frame of his new house. It stood proud against the backdrop of dense forest, just beyond the mission compound's borders. He had learned construction through apprenticeship at Cape Palmas, and now he was enjoying honing these skills. But a bittersweet sense of accomplishment washed over him as he considered the circumstances that led to this moment.

At first, being told to leave the mission grounds hurt. He had seen the disappointment in Lois' eyes, and heard the whispers of the students. But as he worked on this house day after day—a house that would be home to both Mabel and Meissen—he started to see things differently.

There was a time, he remembered with a smile, when he thought the missionaries knew everything. He had thought their new ways, so different, were always better than the old ways of his people. Now, trying to make a life for his two wives and their children, he saw how complicated things could get when two worlds came together. His father had been right when he had insisted all those years ago that going off with the missionaries wouldn't change him. It was impossible to both change and stay the same.

He had changed—in ways no one had predicted. As much as he believed in the hope that Western civilization brought, he cherished the time-honored ways of his people. He knew there was good in both the

Christian teachings and the Grebo traditions, and he knew both ways had their faults.

As he was thinking about this, he heard Old Man Juwillie's voice, "Still trying to have it both ways, I see."

Joseph turned to face Meissen's father and took in the angry look he always wore these days. "Good afternoon, Old Man Juwillie," he said calmly.

Juwillie was wearing the round brim hat Philip Elsea had given him so many years ago when he and Grace first arrived in Kanweaken. The villagers gave the Elseas Kola nut and a white chicken which signifies approval and purity. As Joseph remembered that exchange, it was like looking back on a simpler, more innocent world.

Juwillie looked at the half-built house with disgust. "You think you can change how things look on the outside of your house and everything will be fine with God?"

Joseph took a deep breath, considering his words.

"Remember what Elsea said," Old Man Juwillie said mockingly, "that God you believe in looks on the inside." He was quoting a phrase that Philip Elsea had been fond of repeating, and the memory made Joseph smile despite the tension in the air. "You can't fool God.

He'll know you have two women in there, and neither of them Christian wives."

"I'm not trying to hide anything, Old Man," Joseph said. "I'm just trying to take care of *all* of my responsibilities as well as I can."

Old Man Juwillie walked away, and Joseph went back to work, the sound of his hammer again filling the air. Someday his children would live in a Liberia where people didn't have to choose between the old ways and the new. A place where the wisdom of the elders could live alongside new understandings about how the world worked and how to live a good, moral life.

He deeply regretted that his actions had deprived Mabel of the Christian wedding she'd so hoped for. He knew that she suffered, though she would never show it, and she certainly never complained. However, the past could not be changed. All he could do now was try to make the best life he could for his family and continue working toward a better future for his people.

The months that followed the births of Joseph's first two children were among the most joyful of his life—and then the darkest. Joy turned to ashes as one after the other, both infants slipped away.

Joseph was walking to the market in Kanweaken when he spotted Juwillie on the narrow trail ahead. He caught up with him, and the two men nodded in solemn greeting. Their shared grief had brought a kind of peace between them.

"Joseph," Juwillie said quietly, "I have to confess something to you." He hesitated, then added, "Son."

Joseph turned and looked at the older man. This was the first time he'd called him son since Meissen revealed her pregnancy.

"Do you remember when my aunt came to see the babies?"

Joseph nodded. He recalled the sharp-eyed old woman, her traditional cloth wrap a riot of colors against her skin.

"I remember," Joseph said. "She held our little boy so carefully."

Juwillie's face clouded. "She . . . she performed the throat-widening ritual on them."

Joseph felt the ground drop away beneath his feet, and he almost went to his knees. The throat-widening ritual was an old practice meant to help babies clear their throats so that they would eat more and grow faster. Joseph knew of the practice and realized that might have caused the deaths of his children. "I never thought . . ."

Juwillie shook his head, with sadness on his face.

As they walked in silence, Joseph remembered the babies' struggles to feed, their pitiful cries. It all made terrible sense now. He thought of what he'd learned about infant care from the missionaries. The importance of clean water, of gentle handling. How could this have happened under his roof?

As the initial shock began to fade, Joseph resolved that nothing like this would ever happen again. Not to his family, and not to anyone's. Education became more important than ever.

As they reached the outskirts of the market, with the sounds of haggling and laughter drifting toward them, Joseph turned to Juwillie. "I don't hold you responsible, Old Man Juwillie," he said. "We need to do better. For all our children."

A few months later, Joseph hefted his small bundle of belongings onto his shoulder and took one last look around the little white house he had built just outside the mission compound. His heart felt heavy as he thought of leaving Mabel and Meissen, but there was an opportunity he couldn't allow to pass him by.

Monrovia—the capital city. A place of endless possibilities, or so he had heard. With the war in Europe finally over, missionaries were returning to the Hinterland. Lois didn't need his help as much now that a younger American woman named Anna had joined her.

Trade was opening up, not just for the Congo government and their families, but for everyone. Maybe he could find work there, save up money, and eventually bring his family to join him.

Joseph stepped outside as the sky began to brighten. A moment later, the sun was on full display. When he got to the village center, his cousin Billy Toe and a few other young men were waiting impatiently.

"We almost left without you, Joe!" Billy said with a grin.

Joseph nodded and forced a laugh, trying to match the group's enthusiasm.

As they set off down the path leading northwest toward the coast, Joseph cast one last glance over his shoulder. The thatched roofs of Kanweaken were still visible through the trees. He told himself, as he had told Mabel over and over, "I'll be back before you know it."

But Monrovia was a three-month walk from Kanweaken, and so the men realistically would be gone for more than half a year. They had only been walking for half a day when Joseph, whose steps had been growing slower and slower, finally stopped. "I have to go back."

"You hear your wives calling you?" Billy teased.

Joseph tapped his stomach and tilted his head as if listening to something. He finally said, "Yes, I do. Mabel is calling me."

As it turned out, Billy and the others had a hard time finding work in Monrovia. They met others from farming villages all over Monrovia, and communication was difficult because they spoke so many different languages. "Come back when you know more English," they were told again and again.

The hardships of city life were overwhelming, and the temptation to return to the familiar comforts of Kanweaken grew stronger each day. Many of their peers had already given up, heading back to their villages with tales of the city's cruelties. But despite all the setbacks and challenges, Billy and his companions refused to return to Kanweaken empty-handed.

They knew that returning to Kanweaken would mean facing the disappointment of those who had believed in them. The last words they ever wanted to hear were, "I told you so." The thought of admitting defeat was more daunting than the challenges of Monrovia.

So Billy persevered, taking on any job he could find, no matter how menial or difficult. He worked longer hours than he ever had worked on the farm, slowly improving his English and learning the ways of city life along the way. His resolve was fueled not just by his ambition to improve his own life, but to prove that someone from Kanweaken really could make it in the big city.

As the months turned into years, Billy's persistence began to pay off. He found more stable employment and started to build a network of contacts. Gradually, he was able to rent a small house in the heart of Monrovia, marry a wife, and start a family. What had once seemed impossible was now becoming a reality. Billy was establishing himself in the capital.

His success, hard-won through years of struggle, became a source of pride not just for Billy, but for all of Kanweaken. He had become living proof that their people could thrive in the modern world, and his determination paved the way for many who would follow his footsteps.

Word of Billy's success began to spread back in Kanweaken and the surrounding villages. Soon, others from their home region began to make the long journey to Monrovia, seeking opportunities and a better life. For each of them, Billy's house became their first stop.

Billy's home became the first stop for newcomers from Kanweaken—and even newcomers from nearby villages since Billy was one of the few people who spoke their dialect. His door was always open, and his wife kept a pot of food ready for hungry travelers. Billy would offer advice, share contacts, and sometimes even help find temporary work for those just arriving in the big city.

As more and more people from Kanweaken made their way to Monrovia, Billy's reputation grew. He became a pillar of their community, a link between their rural roots and their urban aspirations.
Even as the years passed and Billy grew older, he never forgot his roots. He continued to welcome people to Monrovia from the next generation and the next.

Though Billy never returned to live in Kanweaken, his impact was felt there too. The money and opportunities he helped facilitate flowed back to the village, gradually improving life for those who remained. Billy had become a bridge between two worlds, helping to shape the future of both Kanweaken and the growing Liberian capital.

06 | JJG

TEACHER JOE

Joseph paced outside their house, listening to Mabel's cries of pain mingled with the encouragement of the village midwife. The humid night air clung to his skin. His heart was racing. They had already lost two babies. Surely fate or whatever God wouldn't be so cruel a third time?

When silence finally fell, it was deafening. Joseph held his breath, straining to hear the cry of a newborn. But there was nothing.

The midwife emerged, her face crumpled. "I'm sorry, Joseph," she said softly.

Joseph stumbled into the house, his vision blurring. There was Mabel, cradling a tiny, still form. In her eyes was a look he had seen twice before, and it shattered his heart anew .He knelt beside her, gently touching the baby's soft cheek. The unfairness of it all threatened to overwhelm him. Three children lost before they had a chance to live.

Later that week, as Joseph stood by the small grave, now the third such tiny mound, he felt a presence beside him. It was Lois, her eyes red-rimmed and weary.

"I'm so sorry for your loss, Joseph," she whispered. Then, something in her seemed to crack. "I'm so tired of seeing babies die. I dream of saving them all. . . . If only I could save one!"

When Mabel's next baby was born, a healthy girl they named Joan, Lois begged to keep her on the mission compound, just for a few months, and give the baby a fighting chance.

Mabel and Joseph agreed, and Lois took Joan up to the mission compound to live with her when she was only a few days old. Mabel's only responsibility as far as the baby's care was to breastfeed her. A good part of Joseph's twenty-two-dollar monthly salary was already going to Lois to pay back the debt for Mabel's dowry. Now that he was paying for Joan's care as well, half of his salary went to the missionary. This arrangement continued until Joan was eight months old, when Lois was called upon to return to the United States to take care of her ailing mother.

With baby Joan back in the arms of her parents, Joseph and Mabel began to reassess their relationship with the mission school. It took students two hours to walk to the mission school from Kanweaken, which wasn't too much farther than many of them ordinarily walked to their mother's farms.

But still, the distance was enough that many children who otherwise would have been ready to begin studying earlier, had to wait until they were older and their parents were willing to allow them to walk that far through the forest without their supervision. By the time they had grown that much, their helping hands were too valuable in the fields.

Joseph often said to Mabel, "What if we had our own school at home in Kanweaken? What if students were able to learn reading and writing right at home? They wouldn't have to worship the Christian God if they weren't ready to."

That was another obstacle for many would-be students from Kanweaken. Parents could see the benefits of learning to read laws and calculate prices to make sure they were getting a fair deal when they went out into the world. Asking their children to take time away from their daily farm chores to pray to a far-off God was, for many, a bigger thing to ask.

Mabel, for her part, firmly believed in the goodness of the Christian God. When she went to church, she could feel things stirring deep in her soul, a presence that Joseph couldn't seem to reach with his analytical mind. She still felt that she had much to learn from Anna, the missionary who remained at the compound after Lois left. But she understood her husband's point of view and knew that, for the sake of the village children, their time was better spent in Kanweaken.

So Joseph, Mabel, and Meissen emptied the wooden-and-mud house Joseph had built and returned home. Kanweaken had gone through rapid changes during those years. Although there still wasn't a road connecting Kanweaken to the cities along the coast, people seemed to be coming and going all the time.

Hut taxes had to be paid in currency now instead of the goods that people usually bartered. This meant that cash crops were becoming as much a necessity as the crops the women grew to sustain their families.

To help their wives and mothers pay these hut taxes, more and more young men went to Monrovia to make their fortunes. Western clothing and goods, traded among the jungle villages, become increasingly commonplace. Square houses made of white-painted boards were starting to replace the round mud huts that Joseph and his generation had been born in.

Joseph built his second wood timber house when they got back to Kanweaken–this one much larger than the first. It had several large rooms for Joan and the rest of the children he and Mabel would have together. Like the missionary compound, Joseph's house was surrounded by a white picket fence.

A wide verandah across the front of the house provided enough room for any child who wanted to learn to come and have lessons. Early every morning, before dawn, the rich, sweet aroma of *fraler*, a sugary pastry that Mabel fried in palm oil, filled the air. Joseph filled a basket with fraler and walked from door to door, gathering up the village children. They followed him and the delicious smells that wafted from his basket back to the house. Soon his wide front porch was filled with rows of children singing their ABCs, reciting multiplication tables, and filling their bellies. Each child had a small blackboard on which they practiced writing and doing sums.

Within the first year, Joseph had to build an addition to his house for all the children who wanted to come and learn. In addition to "learning book," the children learned how to grow nutritious vegetables in the garden, make and mend clothes, construct buildings, and many other skills—all of the things Joseph did in addition to teaching to support his growing family.

Everywhere he went, women found Joseph impossible to resist. His own hometown was no exception. His flirtations and affairs were the subject of countless tales, and it wasn't just idle gossip.[3] As much as Joseph regretted that his obligations to Meissen barred him from giving Mabel the respectable Western marriage she had hoped for, he must have reasoned that the damage was already done and there was no reason not to continue to add to his collection of wives.

Joseph built a hut for Meissen and started a farm that he called Woleken soon after returning to Kanweaken. Meissen had a daughter named Nancy who died in her fifties, and her second daughter Martha lived to her teenage years. Ma Meissen's children included Ada Wesseh, Joseph Geleplay Jr. (deceased), Augustus Thors Geleplay, Sampson (deceased), Esther Beora Dortu, Evelyn, and Martha whose twin brother died as an infant. Then Joseph

---

[3] A family member remembers overhearing one woman joking to another that she wouldn't spoil her reputation for just any man. But if Joe Geleplay made a pass at her? That would be OK!

married his third wife, Esther. She had three daughters named Clara, Annie, and Gwendoline. Wife number four was Jenny, who gave birth to Mary, Sophie (deceased), Moses, Trapitor Mulbah,[4] and Mabel (deceased). Wife number five, Susan, had Elizabeth, Cynthia, and Louise (deceased). If any of these marriages or later affairs hurt Mabel, she was careful not to show it to Joseph.

It was said that Jenny agreed to become Joseph's fourth wife days before the wedding she had planned with another man. She would have been this other man's first wife, a coveted position, but she happily gave that honor up to marry a man who had already committed himself to three other women.

Joseph's popularity with the women caused considerable tension between him and most of the other men in the village. They couldn't stand the way he stole the hearts of the women they loved. It didn't help matters that he was also keeping the children of Kanweaken out of their mothers' fields.

At first the elders didn't pay too much attention to Joseph and his school. They thought it was a novelty that would wear off, similar to the way the zeal that the

---

[4] At the time of this writing, Trapitor Mulbah is fighting for her life due to kidney disease.

missionaries inspired flared up and fizzled out every time they came and went.

But as the years went by, Joseph's school continued to grow. He remembered Lois saying that Liberia's government, under President Tubman, had ordered that funds be allocated to schools all over the country. But because most villages did not know that these funds were available and there was a shortage of qualified teachers, and also because the leadership of the most remote villages were still against education, almost all the money set aside for educating the youth of Liberia never made it outside of Monrovia.

There was no salary for Joseph, so to support his family while teaching, he worked on construction crews, served as the village's tailor, and performed numerous other tasks.

Even though Joseph taught for free, there was still a lot of skepticism about the value of education. Some worried that all education gave young people was the opportunity to turn their backs on Kanweaken and be absorbed into the cities, where they worked too hard for too little and forgot how to work the land. Too many young men had already left for Monrovia now that Liberia was supporting the allied forces in World War

II and was sending its resources to countries all over the world.

Finally, four years after Joseph's school was founded, tensions came to a head. The elders felt they had to address the concerns of parents who complained that their children were spending too much time studying and not enough time planting crops and pounding rice. They ordered Joseph to stop teaching and shut down the school.

The elders continued to pressure him to stop, but the more the conflict over the school simmered, the more children seemed drawn to Joseph's lessons. Young people were particularly captivated by Joseph's stories of his time on the coast with the missionaries.

Eventually, the elders took more drastic action. They summoned Joseph and issued an ultimatum: "Close your school. You're making our children lazy and causing them to forget the ways of their ancestors. If you teach again, you will be fined."

Joseph stood tall, his jaw set. The next morning, he unlatched the door to his classroom, and the children streamed in. By midday, the elders had gathered outside the fence, surrounded by the parents of the students. The elders levied their punishment: one cow, a sack of rice, several gallons of palm oil, and other provisions. This was a small fortune by village standards.

Joseph's father, Jimmy, made his way through the crowd and approached the elders. "I will pay my son's debt," he said quietly. "He earns nothing from this teaching."

That night, a knock at Joseph's door jolted him from sleep. The elders stood outside, the moon shining behind them.

"My father is paying the fine," Joseph said. "He already brought in some of the goods, and he will bring the rest tomorrow."

It was Old Man Juwillie who thrust a torch into Joseph's hands. "Leave Kanweaken," he growled. "Do not return, or you will face worse than fines."

Joseph's fingers tightened around the rough bark of the torch, its flame casting flickering shadows across the faces of the elders. Their eyes, which he usually saw as warm with the wisdom of years, now glinted cold and hard in the flickering light.

"Leave Kanweaken," one of them said threateningly. "And do not return, or you will face worse than fines."

As the elders melted back into the darkness, Joseph stood rooted to the spot, the torch sputtering in his grip. His heart pounded. The smell of freshly rain-soaked earth and the familiar night sounds of the village—the distant lowing of cattle, the chirp of insects, the rustle of palm fronds in the breeze—suddenly sounded incredibly sweet, like nothing he would ever hear anywhere else.

He turned and faced the house he'd built with his own hands. Inside, Mabel and Joan slept, unaware of how their lives had just changed.

How had it come to this? He had only wanted to bring light, to open doors for the children of Kanweaken. To give them the tools to navigate a world that was changing whether they wanted it to or not. Yet here he stood, branded as a threat to the very community he devoted his life to.

As the pale light of dawn began to stretch across the sky, Joseph heard familiar footsteps approaching. He turned to see his parents, their faces etched with concern and something else—a resignation that made his heart constrict.

"It's time to stop, Joseph," his father pleaded. "The village has become so divided."

Joseph opened his mouth to protest, but the words died on his lips as he saw the pain in his mother's eyes.

"We can see how much the children benefit from all you're teaching them," Catherine said softly. "We know that in the future it will all prove to be worth the effort. But for now, the cost is too much."

Her gentle words, so firmly spoken, cut deeper than the elders' threats. Joseph felt the weight of generations pressing down upon him—the traditions that had sustained his people for centuries, the uncertain future that loomed before them, and his own burning desire to bridge that chasm.

Back inside the house, Joseph stood, surrounded by the books and slates that represented his life's work. He spun the globe Lois had given him as a parting gift for the children of Kanweaken. How could he abandon these children who thirsted for knowledge? How could he turn his back on the vision he himself had given them?

07 | 🎴JG

OUTCAST

T he forest swallowed Joseph as he left Kanweaken behind. The dense canopy above filtered the morning light, casting dappled shadows on the narrow path before him. The weight of his meager possessions in a bundle on his back was nothing compared to the burden of uncertainty that pressed upon his heart. How would he care for his wives and children now?

As he walked, memories of his life played through his mind like scenes from a story. The astonishment of his parents when he'd first learned to read. The warmth of Mabel's smile as she played with baby Joan. The chorus of young voices as children eagerly recited their lessons on his porch.

The walk to Tiehnpo was long and arduous. Joseph's feet ached, and his throat grew parched as the day wore on. He hadn't been to Tiehnpo in many years, but he remembered Lois saying that they had requested a school, and Marcy had talked about how much the people loved hearing Bible stories when he traveled through on his preaching circuit. It was a larger village than Kanweaken, and surely there would be at least a few open hearts and minds. Before Joseph got to Tiehnpo, he passed through Dowehken, where after hearing his story, the elders offered him a parcel of land to build a school and his house. He respectfully turned down the offer because he wanted to go as far away as he could from Kanweaken.

Two women working in a rice paddy paused in their labor as Joseph approached and regarded him with weary curiosity. Joseph straightening his posture.

"Good evening," he called out in Grebo, hoping his dialect wasn't too different from theirs. "I am Joseph Geleplay, Teacher Joe from Kanweaken. I've come to ask your chief for a place to sleep tonight." He decided not to say any more just yet.

The women exchanged glances, then smiles.

"Welcome, Joseph Geleplay," the older of the two women said. "What brings you out this way?"

Joseph took a deep breath, choosing his words carefully. "I am a teacher," he said. "I believe that knowledge is the key to our people's future. But not everyone in Kanweaken shares this vision. I've come seeking a place where I might continue my work."

The woman's eyebrows rose slightly. "We have heard of you, Joseph Geleplay," she said. "But it's not for me to decide whether our village needs a teacher."

The aroma of palm butter with salted beef wafted through the air as Joseph followed the women into the village. His stomach growled. He saw that Tiehnpo had not hemorrhaged as many of its young men to Monrovia as Kanweaken had. Most of the village dwellings were still mud huts. Only a few wooden buildings had been constructed at the outskirts.

Tiehnpo, the home of the Paramount Chief, was doing well. It hadn't been forced to hurry into the new Western ways as quickly as other villages had, likely because it had plenty of support from the surrounding villages that answered to the Paramount Chief, and so it had plenty of resources to pay its hut taxes.

Joseph spoke to the elders of the changes that had come to the coastal villages, were making their way through Kanweaken, and would soon change life here too. He leaned forward as he spoke, his eyes bright. "That's why we must learn. Knowledge is our bridge to the new world that is now being created."

To the young people, he said, "Do you want to go to Monrovia too and get some of those good jobs? Send money back to your parents and wives so they can live comfortably?"

When they answered yes, he said, "You better learn to read and do numbers first! You will be alone in that big city, and your neighbor's food will smell so good if you don't have any!"

The elders of Tiehnpo agreed that Joseph would build a school. Joseph sent word to Kanweaken to the boys who helped him with the school he started there, and eleven boys joined him: Johnny P. Weah, Jacob S. Matthew, James C. Nyeneh, Gray T. Alfred, Bennie C. Toe, Brown B. Keh, Daniel P. Keh, Sampson W. Walker, Amos C. Juwillie, Willie W. Welleh, and James Nyepleh Dweh. Soon the familiar sounds of hammers striking wood and the scrape of shovels digging into the earth filled the air.

Soon, Joseph was teaching again, and his school flourished. Within a year, his students were reading simple texts, performing basic calculations, and eagerly absorbing information about the wider world. The school building, at first a novelty, quickly became a hub of village life.

Mabel and the children joined Joseph in a new house he built himself as soon as the harvest was finished. But it wasn't all smooth sailing. As in Kanweaken, many elders grumbled about time wasted on "foreign nonsense" when there were crops to tend and game to hunt. Joseph countered this by integrating practical skills into his lessons. He taught them tips and tricks of farming techniques he'd learned at Kanweaken, and he shared practices he had learned from Lois that reduced infant mortality, always careful to protect the kernel of wisdom in traditional practices while introducing new ways.

One evening, as Joseph pored over his makeshift lesson plans by lamplight, the Paramount Chief appeared at his door.

"You've brought much to Tiehnpo," the chief said, his tone unreadable. "But some fear we're losing our way."

Joseph set down his pen, choosing his words carefully. "Change is coming, whether we like it or not. I only aim to give our people the tools to navigate it on their own terms."

He thought but didn't say out loud, *The only reason your village has avoided change for so long is because you're able to spread the burden to all the other villages in the district.*

The chief nodded slowly. "Perhaps. But remember, Joseph Geleplay, the roots of a tree run deep. Pull too hard, and the whole forest may come down."

Not long after, a group of government officials arrived. Joseph took in their crisp uniforms and stern faces. They were tax collectors who had come to collect the funds the Paramount Chief had collected from all the other villages.

The lead official, a corpulent man with beady eyes, was mid-sentence as Joseph approached. ". . . and furthermore, this district has been delinquent in its contributions to the national development fund."

Joseph stepped forward, switching to his most formal English, "Excuse me, sir. I'm Joseph Geleplay, the schoolteacher here. Perhaps I can be of assistance? I haven't heard of this national development fund. Can you tell me about it?"

The man eyed Joseph suspiciously. "And what exactly do you teach in this . . . school?"

"Reading, writing, arithmetic," Joseph replied evenly, "and an understanding of our rights and responsibilities as Liberian citizens."

A tense silence fell over the gathering. The official's eyes narrowed, but Joseph held his gaze steadily.

Finally, the man cleared his throat. "Well, Mr. Geleplay, since you seem so well-informed, perhaps you can explain to these people the importance of prompt tax payment."

Joseph nodded, then turned to address the villagers in Grebo. "Before we pay these men, we have the right to know exactly what's being asked and how it will benefit us."

He turned back to the official. "Sir, I believe there's been a misunderstanding. We'd be happy to review any official documents detailing our obligations."

The official sputtered, clearly unprepared for such a response. His composure cracked further as he realized the villagers were now watching him expectantly, no longer intimidated by his uniform and blustering manner.

Once Joseph had read the paperwork he insisted on seeing, the officials left with significantly less than they'd demanded. As their truck disappeared down the rough road, a cheer went up from the villagers.

The Paramount Chief clapped Joseph on the shoulder. "It seems your 'foreign nonsense' has its uses after all, teacher."

That evening, as word of the encounter spread, more parents brought their children to enroll in Joseph's school. Even some of the most skeptical elders nodded approvingly as they passed.

Joseph's success with the government officials brought unexpected consequences. Word spread rapidly through the region about the educated man in Tienpo who stood up to authority. Soon, people from neighboring villages began to arrive, seeking Joseph's educated advice on various matters.

One morning, a group of women from a nearby village approached Joseph as he prepared for his classes.

"Teacher," their leader said, her voice urgent, "we've heard you can read the government's papers. Our elders signed an agreement with a company. Now strange machines are tearing up our farmland. Can you help us understand what's happening?"

Joseph examined the document they produced. His brow furrowed as he deciphered the dense legal language. "This grants the company rights to your land for fifty years," he explained, "but there are provisions here for compensation that don't seem to have been honored."

Joseph spent the next hour explaining the contract's terms and discussing potential courses of action.

As soon as the women left, Mabel approached Joseph. "You missed breakfast again," she said, handing him a bowl of cassava and leftover palm butter stew.

Joseph ate quickly, aware that his waiting students would be taken out to the fields without the opportunity to show him the sums they'd done on their slates if he didn't hurry.

That evening, instead of the usual lesson, Joseph led his older students in a discussion about land rights and corporate responsibility. The questions flew and debates grew animated as the students began to finally connect the abstract concepts Joseph talked about with real issues in their communities.

Joseph had thought Tiehnpo would be different from Kanweaken, more open to his ideas about education and progress, since it was the village of the Paramount Chief and more connected to Monrovia. For a while, it seemed he was right. But as the days passed, Joseph began to sense an undercurrent of resentment. The admiration that grew for Joseph among most of the village engendered envy in others.

Whispers reached his ears, such as "How dare this stranger come to our village and take over?" and "He's not even from here, and now he's ruling our boys?" He tried to reassure himself that this was just a vocal minority, that most of Tiehnpo appreciated what he and Mabel were doing for their children.

But the whispers grew louder, and Joseph couldn't shake the feeling that something was brewing. He noticed how some of the men would glare at Mabel when she walked by, how conversations would stop abruptly when he approached. A gnawing worry began to grow in the pit of his stomach.

One afternoon, Mabel went with some of the village girls to fetch water from the river. Joseph watched them go, feeling an inexplicable sense of unease. He knew the spot well. A huge rock jutted out over the water where the children dared themselves to play, believing it was a meeting place for witches.

Hours later, a commotion erupted in the village. Joseph's heart raced as he ran toward the sound, somehow knowing it involved Mabel. The story tumbled out in fragments. Six men appearing from under the water, the girls fleeing in terror, Mabel left behind, found unconscious.

Joseph's world narrowed to a pinpoint as he pushed through the crowd to find his wife. She lay still on the ground, surrounded by people chanting and applying herbs. Time seemed to stretch endlessly as he waited, praying to every god he knew for her to open her eyes.

When Mabel finally regained consciousness, relief washed over Joseph like a wave. But as she recounted what had happened, his relief turned to anger. This was no accident, no simple mishap. The fact that one of the men had been recognized confirmed his worst fears. This had been a deliberate attack.

As word spread to Kanweaken, Joseph found himself torn. Part of him wanted to join the battle party that was forming, to seek revenge for this assault on his wife. But he knew that violence would only beget more violence. Instead, he focused on caring for Mabel and cooperating with the investigation.

When news came that Mabel was recovering and that justice was being pursued through proper channels, Joseph felt relief that bloodshed had been avoided along with gratitude for the support from Kanweaken. The village that had disowned him now had his back again. Tiehnpo, the place he had hoped would be a fresh start, would never be home.

As Mabel recuperated, Joseph considered that their time in Tiehnpo might be coming to an end. Once again, he found himself facing the prospect of uprooting their lives, of seeking a new place where they could pursue their dreams of education and progress without fear. But where would they go?

Joseph taught his students much more than reading, math, and other basic skills. He introduced them to the concept of an entire globe covered with different lands and peoples. He impressed upon them a sense of their own national identity through the celebration of Liberia's Flag Day. He began by describing the grand celebrations in Monrovia that he had only heard about, his voice and gesturing hands painting vivid images in the children's minds of marching bands, crisp uniforms, and proud salutes.

"What is Liberia?" the youngest children asked. They had heard of Monrovia, but what was this country that both Tiehnpo and Monrovia were part of?

Joseph spent weeks preparing his students. He taught them about the flag's meaning, the red and white stripes, and the blue canton with a single star. Unable to procure real uniforms, Joseph's creativity shone through. He fashioned hats from large leaves, shaping them to mimic the boat-shaped military caps worn in Monrovia.

When August 24, Liberia's Flag Day, arrived, Tiehnpo woke to an atmosphere of excitement. The children, dressed in their best clothes with their leaf-hats perched proudly on their heads, gathered outside the school. Joseph had them line up in formation, just as he'd heard the schools in Monrovia did.

The parade began, with Joseph leading his students through the village. They marched with precision, their backs straight and heads held high. At intervals, they would stop, and Joseph would call out commands. The children would salute, their movements crisp and synchronized.

As they marched, they sang the patriotic songs Joseph had taught them: "Parade, parade, parade, parade, we are Gbeapo Central School marching through your town." Their young voices filled with pride for a country many of them were just beginning to understand. Handmade flags waved in the air, adding splashes of red, white, and blue to the green landscape.

The villagers of Tiempo watched in awe, many seeing such a display for the first time. And it wasn't just Tiehnpo that witnessed this spectacle. Word spread as the students marched from one village to another, and people from neighboring villages gathered to see them. When they arrived in Kanweaken, they orchestrated a more elaborate display. All the people came out to see Joseph's Flag Day celebration.

The Kanweaken onlookers were particularly impressed. They watched as Joseph expertly guided the children through their routines, explaining the significance of each movement and symbol to the gathered crowd. Many whispered among themselves, marveling at what a son of their village had accomplished.

The celebration concluded with Joseph giving a rousing speech about Liberian pride and unity. The Kanweaken elders were so filled with regret that they couldn't face Joseph. They had driven this talented young man away, and now he was doing such remarkable things for another village!

One humid afternoon, Joseph headed out to tend the small garden behind his house. This was usually a solitary activity, but he could see that he was about to be joined by a group of teenage boys and the Paramount Chief himself.

"I'll show you where I found it!" one of the boys was saying. He was holding aloft a small green sprout with thick leaves. Joseph's heart sank when he realized what it was. It was a bean seedling.

"Who has done this?" the chief demanded, his voice trembling with anger and fear. "Who has brought this curse upon us?"

"I found it right there!" The boy shrieked. "Right there in Teacher Joe's garden!"

Joseph pushed through the crowd that was growing around the scene. "It's a bean plant," he said calmly, "and it is not mine."

"Yes, it is a bean plant. Don't you know our laws, teacher? Planting beans brings misfortune to the whole village. It is forbidden!"

Joseph opened his mouth to argue. He had no idea where the bean plant had come from. Both he and Mabel knew better than to stir things up. What he did know was that he wouldn't be able to convince anyone this was true. This wasn't a matter of logic or education that beans brought bad luck was a deeply held belief, as real to them as any fact he taught in his classroom.

"Where was it found?" Joseph asked, his mind racing.

"In your yard, teacher," the boy pointed to a bare patch among potato roots where a small plant had been pulled.

"That's impossible," Joseph protested. "I would never . . ." He knew as well as anyone that beans were forbidden. The people of Tiehnpo believed they could cause crop failure, illness among the livestock, and worse.

The chief's voice cut through Joseph's thoughts. "You've brought this on us, teacher. With your foreign ways and strange ideas. Now we see the true cost of your 'knowledge.'"

Joseph looked around at the faces of his neighbors, his students. The trust he'd worked so hard to build was crumbling before his eyes. In that moment, he realized that all his learning, all his good intentions, meant nothing in the face of such deeply rooted fear.

The crowd's murmurs were now growing hostile. Joseph knew his time in Tiehnpo had come to an end, unexpected as it was. That one bean seedling! Such a small and harmless thing, but it had undone all of his work here.

Joseph was compelled to leave Tiehnpo because the offense was impossible to overlook. With a heavy heart, he gathered Mabel and the children and left as quickly as possible.

Kanweaken, including the elders who had driven him away two years earlier, welcomed Joseph and his family with open arms, and soon his school was in full swing. There was no money in Kanweaken for a teacher's salary, so Joseph taught for free. He and Mabel planted a big garden filled with various kinds of fruits and vegetables—potatoes, cassava, greens, eggplant, carrots—and yes, beans. They also harvested rice from Mabel's farm, which they sold at the village market.

With the proceeds, Joseph made sure that every student had the necessary school supplies. He sewed uniforms for the students and made sure each one had a nourishing meal. He felt that with their basic needs met in the present moment, they would be better able to focus on learning for the future.

The following year, after the incident with the beans that brought Joseph back to Kanweaken, the village eagerly anticipated their own Flag Day celebration. Joseph, though still hurt by the deception that had forced his return, threw himself into the preparations with characteristic dedication.

This time, with a full year preparing and the backing of his home village, Joseph created an even more impressive display. The children of Kanweaken, many of whom had witnessed the previous year's celebration, were especially enthusiastic.

On August 24, 1961, Kanweaken was transformed. The parade was larger, the songs louder, and the pride palpable. Joseph had even managed to create simple uniforms, dyed in patriotic colors. Everyone was making the leaf-hats now. They had become something of a local tradition.

As the children marched through Kanweaken, performing the military-style drills Joseph had taught them, the villagers swelled with pride. Even those who had been skeptical of Joseph's methods couldn't deny the power of seeing their children so disciplined and proud.

The celebration culminated in a grand display in the village center, with Joseph leading the children in a final salute to the Liberian flag. As the makeshift band played and the flags waved, many in Kanweaken realized just how much Joseph's vision and dedication had brought to their village. The flags became a symbol of a future where Kanweaken, not yet a dot on the official maps, was a vital part of Liberia.

As the parade dispersed, Joseph noticed two neighbors who hadn't spoken in years exchanging surprised greetings. These men hadn't spoken in years, not since a bitter dispute over a borrowed machete that was lost in the weeds of the jungle and never returned. Yet here they were, caught up in the moment, laughing together at the children's antics. It wasn't much, just the weight of their old grudge momentarily lifted, replaced by the simple joy of a shared new experience.

Many years later, after Joseph had passed, his daughter Ethel met the boy—now a grown man—who had been the source of those ill-fated bean seeds. They were gathered in someone's home to celebrate a wedding. Ethel excused herself to go into another room, but she could still hear the conversation.

She heard the man say that he had gone with Joseph when he started the school in Tiehnpo. When he received word that his mother back in Kanweaken was ill, he promptly went home to see her. To his confusion, his mother wasn't ill at all.

The elders then called him and gave him a handful of bean seeds and told him to plant them in Joseph's garden. They had heard about all the good things that happened for the people in Tiehnpo as a result of Joseph's work, and they wanted him back.

They couldn't admit to Joseph, a younger man, that they had been wrong to send him away. This was why they devised this trick to get him to come home.

08 | JG

BUILDING THE FUTURE

The sun was setting over Kanweaken as Joseph made his way from Mabel's cassava field toward the elders' meeting place in the center of the village. The village had changed significantly since his return. His heart ached as he passed by fields where women toiled alone.

As he walked, Joseph rehearsed his proposal for the elders. A proper school could change everything. It could bring new life to Kanweaken. Students would come from all around, like they did to Tiehnpo. Small businesses might spring up to serve the school community, such as a kitchen to serve school lunches and a tailor to sew school uniforms. *We would be creating new jobs right here in Kanweaken to keep our young people at home.*

He imagined future generations of Kanweaken children, their heads filled with valuable knowledge about how the world worked. *No more being cheated by mining companies or ignored by the central government*, he thought.

The image of lush farmland surrounding the school filled his mind. *We'll grow our own food, teach practical skills alongside book learning. It's the perfect blend of old ways and new.*

Joseph smiled then, thinking of how the school so many feared would replace the village's traditions could actually become a guardian of their heritage. *We'll teach our own language and stories alongside English and mathematics. Our children will never forget who they are.*

Joseph continued walking. In the village now, wooden houses with tin roofs now outnumbered the mud huts by about three to one. Many of the newer huts had straight walls and four corners, with tin roofs instead of thatch. At the same time, the village felt smaller. So many of the younger generation were now starting new lives in Harper and Monrovia.

He recalled what Lois had said about President Tubman. She was there at the beginning of his term, waiting for transportation from Monrovia to Harper. She said that he spoke of a vision of a unified Liberia, with places at the table for all of the nation's tribes. *Perhaps if we show initiative, the government will even support us with resources. Monrovia has taken so much from us, maybe now it will finally start to respect us and give something back.*

A flicker of worry crossed his mind as he remembered rumors of land grabs in other villages. *This school could protect our land, give it a purpose those in power can't ignore.*

Finally, he allowed himself to dream of Kanweaken's future prominence. *A respected school could put us on the map, make us a model for other villages that would follow our example.*

Joseph was at the village center now. Taking a deep breath, he steeled himself for the conversation he was about to initiate. He knew the elders might be skeptical, but he believed in his vision, and he had to try to get them to see it too.

Joseph's palms were damp as he approached the elders' meeting place. He took a deep breath, inhaling the familiar scents of wood smoke and palm wine that hung in the air.

The elders sat in a semicircle, their weathered faces expectant. Joseph saw Old Man Juwillie's eyes narrow slightly as he took his place before them.

"Honored elders," Joseph began, his voice steadier than he felt, "I come to you with a vision for our future." He paused, searching for the right words. How could he make them understand the urgency he felt?

"Our world is changing," Joseph continued. "Every day, more of our young people leave for Monrovia. They go unprepared, easy prey for those who would exploit them."

A murmur rippled through the group.

Joseph said more quietly, "Whether we think they're right to go or not, we can't stop them. All we can do is prepare them and then hope they come back stronger and wiser than when they left."

"How do you propose we prepare them?" one elder asked.

"With your blessing, I propose setting aside some land for a school, under my protection. With land dedicated to a school, and farmland that is worked to support that school, we can ensure we always have a place for our youth to learn. This will be a place where our children can learn to read contracts—and maybe even practice law themselves. They will learn to understand the workings of the government, and they will have a voice in that government so they can protect our way of life."

Joseph's mind flashed to the faces of his own children and to the students who gathered on his porch each morning. He thought of the pride he felt when they mastered a new concept, the hope it gave him for their future.

"This school," he said, his voice growing stronger, "won't just be about book learning. We'll teach our traditions too. Our children will learn to farm smarter, not just harder. They'll understand how to succeed in this new world without losing who they are."

As he spoke, Joseph felt the tension in his shoulders ease. This wasn't just about him anymore. It was about all of them, about the legacy they would leave. "Think of it," he continued more softly. "Years from now, when outsiders come with their contracts and machines to tear up the land, our grandchildren will be ready. They will make us proud."

Joseph stood back when he had finished speaking and waited quietly. The elders exchanged glances. Old Man Juwillie was standing slightly apart, looking thoughtful. In the distance, a child's laughter rang out, a reminder of all that was at stake.

After a long silence, the village chief spoke. "This is an unusual plan, Joseph Geleplay." No other village that we know of has made an arrangement like this."

The next day, the elders announced their decision. "We will grant this land to you, Joseph. But with conditions. It must benefit all. It can never be sold. And you must answer to this council for its use."

Joseph nodded solemnly. "You have my word."

As Joseph left for Harper to get the deed drawn up for the land, he felt the burden of his new responsibility. He was now a guardian, a one-man bulwark against all the forces that would exploit their land and people. It was a heavy responsibility, but one he embraced. For the future of Kanweaken—of all Liberia—depended on such acts of foresight and protection.

As it turned out, the magistrates in Harper were unwilling to deed the land to Joseph, a tribal person, so he had to take his case all the way to Monrovia—all the way to the president.

Although this was a much longer journey than Joseph had made in his life so far, it wasn't quite as long as the three-month sojourn he, his cousin Billy, and the others had planned back when he was first married. This was because the network of smooth, graveled roads now extended all the way to Harper, and Joseph rode almost as many miles in vehicles as he walked.

As Joseph traveled, he marveled at the changing landscape. The dense jungle gradually gave way to more open areas, and he began to see more signs of Western influence—telegraph poles, larger buildings, and even the occasional automobile. Each town he passed through seemed a little bigger, a little more "modern" than the last.

Monrovia, when he finally arrived, was a shock to his senses. It was a much larger, denser, dirtier, and busier city than Harper. The contrast between the modern buildings in the city center and the sprawling shanty towns on the outskirts was stark. With every step as he walked down the wide streets, he could smell a different meal wafting from the open windows and doors he passed by. The mix of Western suits and traditional African clothing on the bustling sidewalks fascinated him.

Joseph's impeccable attire set him apart in Kanweaken, but he felt awkward and out of place in the capital. He had an acute awareness of his surroundings, and he sensed the stares directed at him, a rural schoolteacher in a sea of urban sophistication.

His first stop was the famous Waterside Market. He had heard tales of this bustling hub of commerce, but nothing had prepared him for the reality. The market was a riot of color, sound, and activity. Vendors shouted their wares, customers haggled over prices, and the air was thick with the scents of spices, fresh produce, and grilling meat. Joseph marveled at the sheer variety of goods on offer—local fruits and vegetables he recognized from home alongside imported items he had never seen before.

As Joseph navigated his way through the crowded market, he reflected on how it embodied Liberia's growth and changing identity. The market seemed to pulse with the energy of a nation in transition, blending traditional African commerce with the influences of the wider world.

He overheard snatches of conversation about the booming iron ore industry and the influx of foreign investment, topics that seemed far removed from the concerns of Kanweaken but were clearly shaping the future of the country.

At the capitol building, a young man in a Western suit told Joseph he wasn't quite sure how to handle his request, since this kind of thing was normally handled by county governments. Two other people, both equally well-dressed, heard Joseph's story and shook their heads. Finally, someone told him that the only person who could resolve this would be the president. Joseph could make an appointment to see him the next day.

The first thing in the morning, after sleeping in a small room he had rented near the capitol building, Joseph went to an area where he had seen people trading goods and purchased some personal items. Then Joseph made his way to the executive mansion, an imposing structure that seemed to embody the power and aspirations of the young nation. The building's modern architecture and manicured grounds stood in sharp contrast to the simpler government offices in Harper.

As he waited for his appointment, Joseph rehearsed his plea in his head, trying to anticipate any questions or objections the president might raise. The weight of his responsibility to Kanweaken and all the rural communities like it pressed on his shoulders.

Finally, he was ushered into President Tubman's office. The room exuded an air of formal authority that made Joseph acutely aware of his rural origins. President Tubman, known for his preference for protocol and formality, regarded Joseph with curiosity and a bit of impatience.

"Mr. Geleplay," the president said, his voice crisp and authoritative, "what brings you to Monrovia?"

Joseph found President Tubman as Lois had described him a decade ago, curt and efficient, but not unfriendly. He listened to Joseph's story for only a few minutes before waving his hand and asking for the paperwork to sign. "Liberia needs more citizens like you, Joseph," he said. "We need education and opportunities for everyone, from border to border, if we hope to maintain any kind of peace. We cannot survive as a country divided."

"Yes, sir," Joseph said. The tone of his voice conveyed his wholehearted agreement.

"Yes, this country needs more men like you," Tubman said again. "What was the name of your village?"

Joseph described Kanweaken, the little village in the hinterland that missionaries hadn't even reached until 1931. He told the president about people who worked hard and lived simply. Bright children who got up early to "learn book" before helping out on their mother's farms. The worry that kept them awake when they saw other villages disappear thanks to the land grabs of mining companies. The hope and dread that filled their hearts when young men decided to leave in order to keep the bellies of their families full.

"Kanweaken," the president repeated. "Did you know I was born in Harper? But I never ventured very far into the jungle."

Joseph later stood on the bustling streets of Monrovia, watching the Flag Day parade. The red, white, and blue of the Liberian flag fluttered against the backdrop of the capitol's gleaming skyline. The rhythmic thump of drums and the brassy notes of a marching band filled the air, punctuated by the cheers of the crowd.

In the mixed crowd, Joseph saw some in Western suits and some in tribal patterns, a vision of a nation unified. He saw a country that could continue moving forward, overcoming differences between tribes as it strived for equality.

President Tubman's words from their meeting echoed in his ears: "Liberia's disadvantage is that we were never colonized." Joseph disagreed. Their advantage was precisely that—the freedom to forge their own path, to build a nation on their own terms. Joseph returned to Kanweaken with the deed for the land and a guaranteed salary as Kanweaken's school administrator. His eighth-grade education might not sound like much of a foundation today, but it was the average education level among teachers in Liberia at that time.

Fig. 2 – Joseph's government-issued ID card as a School Principal

Joseph heard the machines before he saw them. The low rumble carried through the jungle, setting the village dogs barking and chickens squawking.

"What could this be?" he muttered, following the sound.

At the edge of the clearing, Joseph found half the village already gathered. Huge yellow beasts of metal were tearing through the trees, leaving a wide swath of destruction in their wake. Men in hard hats scurried around the machines like ants, shouting and gesturing.

One of the elders stood at Joseph's elbow, his lip curled. "You knew about this, didn't you, Joseph? This is why you got that deed last year. You must have told them to bring this road when you went to Monrovia."

Joseph shook his head, genuinely surprised. "No, I had no idea. I swear it." But he could see the doubt in the elder's eyes, and in the faces of other villagers.

Days passed, and the road crept right up to the edge of the clearing where most of Kanweaken's huts stood. A few of the village's young men went and asked to join the crew, but they were turned away.

It wasn't long before the men in suits showed up. They came in shiny trucks, all smiles as they talked about the progress the road would bring. Joseph asked one of them, "What is this road for? There are no mines right around here. No plantations either."

"It's for Tubman and his people," the man said. "He's from Monrovia, you know. He wants an overland route to Harper, where he's from."

Joseph had heard that the streets of Harper were paved now. It wasn't just asphalt like most of the streets in Monrovia. Harper's residents walked and drove on real pavement. The city was an island of mansion-style homes, emerald lawns, and wide paved streets surrounded by deeply rutted roads that sent up great plumes of orange dust or splashed mud feet into the air, depending on the season.

"Mr. Geleplay," the man said, eyeing the newly valuable land. "Have you considered what else you could do with this property? There's good money to be made here now, with this road."

Joseph looked at the man, then at the half-built schoolhouse behind him. He thought of the children who crowded his porch every morning, eager to learn.

"This land already has a purpose," Joseph said simply. "It's for the children."

The man in the suit opened his mouth, likely to argue, but Joseph had already turned away. He had work to do. The road was coming whether they liked it or not. Joseph's job now was to make sure Kanweaken met it on its own terms.

09 | 🏛️ JJG

CHILDREN AND GRANDCHILDREN

J oseph stood at the edge of the village, gazing down the long stretch of unpaved road that now connected Kanweaken to the wider world. Though still rough and often treacherous–a muddy quagmire in the rainy season and a dusty, rutted path in the dry–this road had begun to change everything.

It wasn't the steady stream of traffic he had initially imagined. Days could pass with little more than the occasional truck or a regular vehicle lurching its way through. But when travelers did come, their arrival was an event. The village would come alive with excitement, people gathering around to hear news and stories from afar.

These sporadic connections were slowly but surely expanding Kanweaken's horizons. Harper, once a distant and almost mythical place to many villagers, now felt within reach. Even Monrovia, where his cousin

Billy Toe had made his home, seemed less like a far-off dream.

Joseph reflected on how these changes were affecting the village youth. They listened with rapt attention to tales of city life, their eyes shining with ambition.

The road, for all its mud and dust, had brought Kanweaken closer to the pulse of the nation. But it had also made the gaps in their local infrastructure more apparent than ever. Joseph's dream of a high school as a way to keep their brightest youth rooted in the community while preparing them for the wider world felt as urgent as it did impossible.

As Joseph watched his ever-growing family, he marveled at how quickly time had passed. With nearly two dozen children now, ranging from adults starting their own families to toddlers still clinging to their mothers' *lappa*, he felt the weight of responsibility more keenly than ever. Mabel, Joseph's first and most steadfast partner, had borne her last child seven years prior: a daughter she nicknamed "Hard Time."

Mabel's last pregnancy was fraught with complications from the start. Unlike her previous pregnancies, this one left her bedridden for months, her usually robust frame weakened by constant nausea and fatigue. Joseph had watched helplessly as his wife, normally a pillar of strength, struggled to carry this child to term.

When labor finally began, Mabel was on her farm alone. She stood at the edge of the field with one hand on her back, and the other brushing tenderly over her belly. For weeks she had been confined to the house due to complications of her high-risk pregnancy. But that morning, she woke up feeling more energetic than she had in a while. Maybe it was the fresh air she craved or the need to check her crops, but against all better judgment, she went out to her farm.

Shortly after she arrived, a sudden sharp pain shot through her belly. She gasped, clutching at her side as the pain came again, this time stronger. She knew immediately what it was; this was not her first baby. Panic fluttered in her chest. The next farm, where she could go for help, though not so far away seemed impossible to get to since the baby was not waiting. She could see the outline of the neighbor's hut in the distance, but every step now felt impossible.

Too many babies have been lost already, Mabel thought. Then she remembered what she had in her hut. A knife used for peeling and slicing vegetables. Ah, the quiet, purposeful work of farm life. She crawled to get the knife, raised herself up, leaned back against a tree, spreading her *daju* (the second *lappa* worn by most Greabo women), and did what she had done many times.

Just when it seemed all hope was lost, she felt a shift and a warmth coming out of her body. Her daughter entered the world with a cry that pierced the silence.

Mabel tied the umbilical cord with a string from her *daju*, then cut it and wrapped her in the *lappa*. She held the infant close and wept for joy and for relief as she went back home.

This baby entered the world so small and frail that she could fit in the palm of her father's hand, though Mabel had carried her to full term. The midwife warned Joseph and Mabel not to get too attached, certain the child wouldn't survive the night. But Mabel, exhausted though she was, had looked at the baby and declared, "This one's a fighter. She's my Hard Time, but she'll make it."

Against all odds, the child had clung to life. Those first weeks were a blur of sleepless nights and constant worry. Mabel would sit for hours, cradling their tiny daughter, willing her to grow stronger. Neighbors would visit, expecting to pay their respects to a grieving family. But their daughter continued to live.

As she grew, defying every dire prediction, her nickname stuck. "Hard Time" became a testament to the child's tenacity, a reminder of the struggle she had overcome just to exist.

Fig. 3 – Mabel and Joseph

The experience had changed Mabel. After this birth, she knew her childbearing years were over. There was a finality to the sense that she had been granted this last, precious gift against impossible odds. Joseph saw in Mabel's eyes a new depth of wisdom and gratitude each time she looked at their youngest child.

The realization that his wives were reaching the end of their childbearing years brought Joseph a mix of emotions—a bittersweet acknowledgment of time's passage, but also a renewed focus on the future of all these young lives he had brought into the world—and the grandchildren they had begun presenting him with.

His thoughts often turned to the children who had moved to Monrovia. They sent letters describing their lives in the capital city—how hard they worked, and how much they treasured the small comforts and moments of beauty they created. Joseph read these letters with pride. As glad as he was that they were making their way in the world, he wondered whether Kanweaken would always be home to them. Or would it become a distant memory, a place to visit but never to stay?

Joseph's thoughts lingered on Florence, his second daughter, who had been among the first to leave home for the capital city. Unlike her younger siblings who usually stayed in Monrovia for a year or two, came home for a season, and then went back as if drifting like ghosts between two worlds. But, Florence had remained in the capital, her commitment to the "civilized" life never wavering.

He recalled the day he granted her request to go to Monrovia to become a ward of a Congo family and their servant.

Florence's letters, when they came, were polite and proper, filled with the refined language she had acquired in the city. Yet Joseph sensed an undercurrent of something left unsaid, a distance that went beyond the physical miles separating them. He had heard what life was like for village girls who went to Monrovia and served Congo families, the physical and sexual abuse the girls endured. These stories haunted Joseph.

Word of pregnancy had reached home via family members who had gone to visit Florence, but she never mentioned having a child in her letters. Whenever she visited, which was a rare occurrence, Hard Time remained by her side until she fell asleep. Her friends would gather at her home, eager for her presence, as she recounted captivating tales of Monrovia and the individuals she had encountered.

Fig. 4 – Mabel's and Joseph's children
Left to right: Bertha, Joan, Florence, Victoria, Ethel
Seated: Raymond

The decision had been ambitious, an expression of hope that she might complete a high school education, make a good marriage, and build a comfortable, stable life for herself. Now, years later, Joseph found himself grappling with the consequences of that choice.

Despite the challenges she had faced, or perhaps because of them, Florence had emerged as a fierce advocate for education and independence, especially for her younger sisters. Her letters often contained advice and encouragement for the younger girls in the household, urging them to seize every opportunity for learning and growth.

Joseph admired Florence's resilience, her ability to transform her experiences—both good and bad—into guidance for others. Yet he couldn't help but wonder about the price she had paid for this wisdom. The bright-eyed girl who had left Kanweaken years ago had been replaced by a woman whose poise and sophistication were tempered by a hardness that Joseph found difficult to reconcile.

As he reread Florence's latest letter, Joseph felt a complicated mix of pride in her accomplishments, sorrow for the hardships she had endured, and a lingering uncertainty about whether the path he had chosen for her had truly been the right one. Years had passed since she first left for Monrovia. She was now married, the mother of two small children, and she was on her way home for a short visit.

In the letter announcing her upcoming visit, she had made a logical case for her parents' youngest daughter to come live with her. The girl could help out around the house while going to school.

Joseph looked up from Florence's letter and watched Hard Time play with her siblings in the yard for a few moments. At seven years old, she already showed a maturity that sometimes caught adults off guard. For example, there was the day she refused to join in a game because she believed the rules were unfair. She stood her ground with a stubborn determination that wasn't often seen in one so young. Joseph could already see this little girl growing into a principled, hardworking young adult with a bright future.

The opportunity Florence offered wasn't one he could pass by. He knew that their youngest daughter, their "Hard Time," would make the best of this opportunity and succeed. Starting from birth, she had always fought so hard for her place in the world. Perhaps this "Hard Time" had been preparing her for such a challenge all along. And under Florence's watchful eye, Joseph was certain she would be kept safe from the dangers and traps that waylaid so many other girls.

Joan, Joseph's oldest daughter, had completed eighth grade but had gotten pregnant and then married, settling down in Kanweaken instead of making the trip to Monrovia for high school.

Ethel, his second oldest, had also hoped to go to high school in Monrovia, but life had taken her in another direction too. He remembered the day when a friend of Mabel's had come to their home and admired the smiling baby, who was crawling on her hands and knees at seven months old. So chubby and healthy! "I'm claiming her right now," the woman had said. "She will marry my son as soon as she's grown."

Betrothals like this were taken seriously as a long-standing tradition that cemented bonds among families, keeping the village united and strong. Now, with the benefit of hindsight on the opportunities that had opened up for Ethel's generation, Joseph felt a pang of regret for having allowed such a promise to be made.

As Ethel grew, her intelligence and curiosity had filled Joseph with hope. He had envisioned a future of education and other possibilities for her. But cultural expectations and the weight of that early betrothal had steered her life in a different direction. Before she could finish eighth grade, Ethel was pregnant. The news had hit Joseph hard, a stark reminder of the challenges his daughters faced in a world that cruelly limited their choices.

The situation had become complicated when the young man to whom Ethel had been promised as a baby declared his intention to marry her despite the pregnancy. His family, however, had adamantly refused, viewing the pregnancy as a disgrace. The conflict had escalated, eventually leading Ethel to leave Kanweaken for Yekepa, where Aunty Ida, my dad's sister, took her in and helped her. She eventually married and had more children, making her dream of finishing high school that much more difficult.

As Joseph contemplated Hard Time's potential move to Monrovia, he reflected on the vastly different circumstances of his daughters, born two decades apart. The world had not been ready for the dreams and aspirations of Florence and Joan, and things had been hard for them. He prayed it would be kinder to his youngest.

He marveled at how unique each of his children's journeys would be. Their future was being shaped by circumstances not just in the village but around the world. Leaving the tribe had been almost unheard of when he was born. Now, his children could go live in a city hundreds of miles away. What next?, he wondered. How many generations before his descendants were crossing oceans?

As a father, all he could do was continue to support and encourage them, hoping that the opportunities he provided and the values he instilled in them would help them create meaningful and fruitful lives, wherever they found themselves.

Joseph's children noticed small details about his behavior that spoke volumes. Every night when he came home, no matter how late, one of his wives or daughters was always waiting to serve him a plate of food. Hard Time observed that he never cleared his plate completely at meals, and she asked him why he always left some food behind.

"When somebody serves you," he explained, "you have to be considerate and think about that person. Maybe they have not had anything to eat all day, yet here they are, serving you. You cannot eat up everything without thinking of them. You must always leave something for the one who served you."

Joseph often entertained his children with folktales, each carrying a moral lesson. One story he told was about two girls who encountered a magical creature by a river:

"A humble village girl went to fetch water and met a mermaid-like being who offered to grant her a wish. The girl, overwhelmed, said she didn't know what to ask for. Anything would be fine! The creature took her to an underwater paradise for a week, then sent her home with beautiful jewels and fine things.

When she returned, another girl known for her beauty and vanity heard the tale. Certain that she deserved even greater rewards, this girl went to the river, found the creature, and demanded riches.

The creature nodded and whisked her away. But instead of taking her to the sparkling underwater palace, he took her to a dark miserable place filled with nothing but cold, slimy rocks that were sharp to sit on. She returned empty-handed and humbled." "You see," Joseph would conclude, "we must approach life with humility and gratitude. Never assume that things will be simply given to you."

Other times when he told the story, he said, "Beauty and pride alone will not bring you happiness."

These stories, along with his own lived example, shaped his children's values and worldview. "If you don't stay in school," he would tease, "your neighbor's food will smell that much better because you'll have a hungry belly." When his older daughters married young or became pregnant before finishing school, each setback and lost opportunity pained him deeply.

Meanwhile, the school, Joseph's life's work, was thriving. Students up to the eighth grade were receiving an education that blended traditional knowledge with the skills needed for the modern world. But there was still so much work to do. Without a high school, Kanweaken was still sending its brightest young minds away just as they reached the cusp of adulthood.

The land he had secured for a future high school weighed heavily on Joseph's mind. He knew that building and staffing a high school would require resources far beyond what the village currently had. Yet it was essential for Kanweaken's future.

As Kanweaken slowly changed, Joseph found himself mediating more disputes between the old ways and the new. Young people, inspired by stories from travelers and letters from relatives in the cities, were questioning traditional values more openly. Some elders resisted fiercely, while others looked to Joseph to help navigate this new world. Despite the challenges, Joseph felt a sense of cautious optimism.

The year was 1972, and Liberia had elected a new president, William Tolbert. The messenger who had brought Florence's letter asking for Hard Time had also brought a transcript of the new president's inaugural address.

President Tolbert's words were filled with hope and grand visions for Liberia's future. Joseph was particularly struck by the president's emphasis on youth, education, and rural development—all issues close to his own heart.

As he read, Joseph felt a cautious optimism rising within him. Tolbert spoke of transforming rural areas, of quenching the thirst for knowledge, of industrialization and progress. These were the very things Joseph had been working toward for decades in Kanweaken.

Yet, Joseph had lived long enough to know that grand speeches didn't always translate to real change. He thought back to the promises of previous administrations, promises that had often run out of gas before they ever made any difference in the hinterland. Still, there was something different about Tolbert's tone. He conveyed a sense of urgency and commitment.

The president's words about lifting people from "the darkness of fear, uncertainty, and suspicion" resonated deeply with Joseph. Wasn't that exactly what he had been trying to do through education? To give people the tools to shape their own destinies?

As he finished reading, Joseph sat back in his chair, lost in thought. If even a fraction of Tolbert's vision came to pass, it could mean tremendous opportunities for Kanweaken and villages like it across Liberia. Perhaps, he mused, the timing was right to push harder for that high school. Perhaps it was time for another visit to Monrovia.

He looked out his window at the village he had devoted his life to. In the distance, he could hear the sounds of children playing, their laughter carrying on the evening breeze. He smiled, allowing himself to imagine the bright futures Tolbert had spoken of. Whatever came, Joseph knew he would continue working to make that vision a reality for Kanweaken.

10 | ﹒JJG

THE PATH TO CONGRESS

J oseph sat on his verandah a week later, the newspaper article about Tolbert's inaugural address spread before him. The president's words about a unified Liberia, with opportunities for all citizens regardless of tribal background, stirred something deep within him. But it was the announcement of open congressional elections that truly captured his attention. Any citizen of Liberia was welcome to register as a candidate, regardless of birth or background.

On one hand, a position in Congress could give Joseph the power to effect real change. He could fight for better schools, improved infrastructure, and fair treatment for the hinterland communities. He imagined standing in the halls of power in Monrovia, advocating for the needs of people who had so long been ignored.

But he would have to win an election first. How would he campaign across such a vast area? The logistics alone were daunting, since many of the villages still didn't have roads and could only be accessed by foot. He wasn't sure how big Karforh District was, but he knew it easily covered a thousand square miles. He would miss his family. And how would his students do without him?

When Mabel voiced these same concerns that had already crossed his mind, he said, "All I can do is try. There's no glory at all if I don't at least try." The first step would be to go to Monrovia and register. That was simple enough.

The next day, the village elders came to the school with a letter from a corporation seeking to buy the school land for a pitifully small amount. The letter was addressed to the village leadership, not to Joseph, who still held the deed. "Maybe that paper's no good now," one elder said. "That old president signed it, and we have a new president now."

"I'll straighten it out with the new government," Joseph said. "I'm going to Monrovia anyway."

That night, Joseph outlined his campaign plans in his head. He would start by traveling to key villages, gauging support and building a network of allies. He would focus on visiting market towns on busy days to reach people from multiple villages at once. He would need to craft a message that resonated beyond Kanweaken, addressing the shared struggles of rural communities across the region.

As he prepared for bed, Joseph found himself energized by this new challenge. The people of Kanweaken had been patiently sending tax money to Monrovia for decades now. Finally they would have representation.

Monrovia, when Joseph arrived, was filled with new energy in the wake of Tolbert's inauguration. The streets and markets were alive with discussions of the new administration's promises and plans.

Registering as a candidate was more straightforward than he had anticipated. As he filled out the necessary forms, a young official named Samuel, who introduced himself as one of Tolbert's new appointees, struck up a conversation with him.

"You're the candidate from Kanweaken?" Samuel asked, his eyes lighting up with interest. "President Tolbert has been talking about the need for more representation from the interior. What made you decide to run?"

Joseph explained his background as a teacher and his vision for improving education and infrastructure in the hinterland. Samuel nodded approvingly.

"That's exactly the kind of perspective we need in Congress," he said. "You'll need to build a strong network of supporters across your district."

Joseph nodded. Before he could respond, Samuel continued, "And I know it's not going to be easy, considering how far behind we are with putting in basic infrastructure."

"That's what I am to help change," Joseph said.

"And don't forget," Samuel added, "President Tolbert's Unification Policy isn't just about government jobs. It's about bringing all Liberians into the political process. Your campaign itself, win or lose, will be part of that change."

With his candidacy officially registered, Joseph set out to begin his long road to Congress. He knew it would be challenging, but he was ready to give it his all. Joseph's campaign began in earnest before he had made it all the way home to Kanweaken. He spoke at village gatherings, marketplaces, and anywhere people would listen. His message was simple but powerful: the hinterland deserved a voice in Monrovia.

In one memorable encounter, an elder in a remote village challenged him. "Why should we trust you? You've been teaching our children to leave us."

Joseph nodded, acknowledging the man's concern. He took a moment to gather his thoughts before responding.

"I understand your fears," Joseph began, his voice gentle. "I've seen our young people leave too. But let me ask you this: When the government men come with their papers, wouldn't you like to read those papers yourself? When companies want our land, wouldn't you like your grandchildren to understand the contracts?" The elder's expression softened slightly, but he remained silent.

Joseph continued, "I don't teach our children to leave. I teach them to see. To see the world that's coming, whether we like it or not. And now, I want to go to Monrovia to make them see us. To make them understand our needs, our ways, our wisdom."

He paused, then added, "Think back to when we were young. Remember how the foresters, the mining companies, and the rubber plantations would come and snatch up our youth? Those young people were taken by force, or they left out of necessity. There were too many hungry bellies to feed. Those boys rarely came back. And when they did, they were broken. They had nothing to bring home but shame."

The elder nodded solemnly, his eyes darkening with the somber memories.

"But now," Joseph said, his voice growing passionate, "when our educated youth leave, it's by choice. They go with knowledge, with skills. And yes, some may stay away, but many come back. They bring new wealth, new ideas, new ways to help our community grow stronger. They build bridges between our world and the world beyond."

He gestured to the village around them. "This is our home. It will always be our home. But the world beyond is changing. We need a voice in that change. Someone who knows our ways, who will fight for our interests. That's why I'm running. Not to take our children away, but to bring the power of knowledge home to us, and to ensure that when our children do leave, they do so on their own terms, with the ability to return and enrich our community."

The elder considered Joseph's words for a long moment. Finally, he nodded. "You speak with wisdom, teacher. But remember, if we send you to Monrovia, you go to speak for us, not for yourself."

"I give you my word," Joseph replied solemnly. "Your voices will be heard. I will work to create a Liberia where our children can choose to stay or go, but always have a home to return to."

The campaign trail was grueling. Joseph slept in strangers' homes, ate whatever was offered, and battled the elements. The rains turned roads into quagmires, delaying his journey between villages for days at a time.

As the election neared, he sensed the tide turning against him. His opponent, an Americo-Liberian backed by powerful interests in Harper, had resources Joseph couldn't match. His promises of immediate development projects, as empty as those promises were sure to be, swayed many voters.

Joseph didn't win that first election, but he had learned so much that he was confident he would win the next time.

Joseph's second campaign for Congress began with high hopes. He had learned from his first attempt and built a strong network of supporters, particularly among the younger generation who appreciated his progressive views on education. But he soon found himself caught between the traditional power structures and his own personal complications.

The village elders had not forgotten about the five hundred acres. What Joseph saw as legally purchased land for development and education, they viewed as a challenge to their traditional authority over land distribution. Their opposition took subtle but effective forms.

When Joseph arrived in a village to campaign, he often found the meeting hall mysteriously occupied by a suddenly called traditional ceremony. In some places, families who might have hosted him were quietly advised that doing so would be "unwise."

The whispers started small but grew. "How can he represent our traditions in Monrovia when he won't respect our wishes about our own land?" The elders were skilled at spreading such messages without appearing to campaign against him directly. They suggested that his refusal to return the undeveloped portions of the land showed he cared more about personal gain than community needs.

Joseph's personal life provided additional fuel for his opponents. His natural charm and progressive ideas made him popular with women, including wives and girlfriends of influential men. His reputation for attracting women created enemies. When his first son was born to a woman who wasn't one of his wives, though he acknowledged and supported the child, it gave his opponents another weapon.

"How can we trust him to fight for our interests in government," one elder asked at a crucial community meeting, "when he fights us over our land and disrupts our families here?" The fact that the elder's own wife had been seen frequently at Joseph's campaign meetings went unmentioned.

Some community leaders sided with Joseph, including one respected elder named Tom Nimely Slobert. The town chief at the time, he stood up at a contentious meeting to declare, "We cannot falsely accuse this man. He bought the land fairly. We signed the papers ourselves." But such voices were overwhelmed by the quiet but persistent campaign against him.

Village by village, Joseph found his support eroding. Women still came to his campaign meetings in large numbers, but their husbands and fathers increasingly opposed him. Young people were enthusiastic about his educational vision but were warned by their elders not to support him.

The elders sent intermediaries suggesting they would cease their opposition if he returned the undeveloped land, but Joseph refused to be pressured.

He believed in his plans for schools and development, and he knew the land had been legally purchased. This principled stance cost him the election, but it preserved his integrity and his vision for the future.

The defeat was bitter, but it taught Joseph valuable lessons about power, tradition, and the need to balance progress with respect for established authorities. These lessons would serve him well in his third and finally successful campaign for Congress.

The third time Joseph ran for Congress, two years later, he worked even harder. When he visited villages to ask the people for their votes, he didn't just give a speech and leave. He stayed for several days and made sure everyone who was willing to listen understood how much good he could accomplish when he went to work for them in Monrovia.

He listened to families talk about land disputes with mining and timber companies and about how difficult it was for farmers to produce enough food, not to mention cash crops, with so much of the younger generation leaving for the city.

He told stories about villages closer to Monrovia that had started getting tax money back from the Tolbert administration so that they could build their own schools and improve their own roads.

"Schools and roads," Joseph said to a growing crowd of villagers in Tabaken at the end of a long market day. "You want your own school, like so many other villages have, and you want a good road so people can get to it. A school here would look good, help this place grow and become a town, not just a village."

Heads nodded. "That would bring the young people back," someone said.

"Do you know what a school would do for Tabaken, that's even more important?" Joseph paused and looked into the expectant faces around him. Then he continued, "Two months ago, representatives from a logging company visited Feloken. They brought contracts written in English that nobody there could read. The chief sent a messenger to fetch me. I read those contracts and saw that they were offering one-tenth of what the timber was worth."

"That is not surprising," a middle-aged man in the crowd said. "They do that all the time."

"But here's what matters," Joseph said, his voice growing stronger. "Because those people in Feloken had someone who could read English, who understood contracts, they didn't sign. They negotiated. Today, they're building a new school with the fair payment they received."

A woman stepped forward, her chin raised. "And if we send you to Monrovia, you'll read our contracts too?" A few people laughed, and the crowd spread out a bit. It would be dark soon.

"I'll do more than that," Joseph replied. "I'll fight for laws requiring contracts to be written in our languages, not just English. I'll push for schools in every village to train students in how this country works, so you can read your own contracts."

A week later, Joseph traveled to a large gathering of Graebo elders in Tiehnpo. He arrived on foot, passed on the dusty road by his opponent, the same Americo-Liberian who had defeated him before, in a shiny car. As in the last campaign, this veteran politician promised lucrative land development projects that would make everyone rich so they would no longer have to depend on farming.

When it was Joseph's turn to speak, he respectfully addressed each elder by name and asked about particular concerns he remembered each village dealing with. Then he carefully rebutted his opponent's claims. "A certain amount of land development is necessary," he said. "And each village should be fairly compensated when they sacrifice farmland for said development. We should profit from the riches of this country as much as anyone. But," he said, smiling, "everyone here knows that we can't eat money. We need farmers. We need to support our farmers, not get rid of them, right? And we need to raise a new generation of farmers. We still need to eat, after all, and so will our grandchildren."

The elders smiled. Joseph's opponent stared at the ground. Joseph had been speaking in Graebo, and the Americo-Liberian didn't understand a word.

"Send me to Monrovia," he said, now in English, "not because I make the biggest promises, but because I know your struggles. I've walked your path, taught your children, stood up for you when Monrovia tried to take too much. And now I'll be your voice in Monrovia—not because I speak the best English, but because I speak your language. I understand the traditional ways we all want to protect, and I share your dreams for our children's future."

This time, the election wasn't even close. Village after village reported overwhelming support for Joseph. His opponent's money and his connections with the spirits couldn't match the trust Joseph had built through patient, persistent engagement with the people.

On the evening of his victory, Joseph sat on his front porch in Kanweaken, receiving a steady stream of well-wishers. Even Old Man Juwillie came to give his blessing.

Joseph had finally won the people's trust. Now he would have to prove worthy of it in the halls of power in Monrovia.

11 | JJG

FAMILY LIFE IN MONROVIA

The taxi wound through Monrovia's streets, its worn suspension absorbing the bumps and dips of the pavement. Joseph watched Mabel's face as she took in the city—the tall buildings, the constant motion, the press of humanity so different from the sights and sounds of Kanweaken. Her expression remained carefully neutral, but he noticed how she gripped the fabric of her *lappa* whenever a car horn blared.

The apartment on Front Street, when they reached it, seemed to shrink under the weight of their expectations. Joseph had visited before, during his campaign, but now he saw it through Mabel's eyes: the narrow stairs and small, empty rooms with paint already peeling from around the windows.

Five grown children of Joseph had come with him from Kanweaken. He had carefully selected them from each wife to represent their mother, just as

Joseph had been selected by the people and sent to represent the district. Clara came from Esther's household, Augustus was Meissen's envoy, and others spoke for their respective mothers. Joseph saw this arrangement as both practical and fair, allowing each branch of his family to maintain a presence in his urban life while ensuring educational opportunities for these chosen children.

It didn't take the children long to explore every inch of the apartment and claim their sleeping places. Then they looked at Mabel, who stood in the modest cooking area, opening and closing cupboard doors.

Joseph knew she was thinking of her outdoor kitchen in Kanweaken, where she could direct the preparation of meals for dozens with the help of Jenny, Susan, and the other wives. Here, the space barely allowed two people to pass each other. Yet he had seen the spark of interest in her eyes when he showed her the electric stove, the refrigerator humming quietly in the corner.

Joseph stood at the window and watched the steady flow of traffic below. The sights and sounds of Monrovia, with its paved streets, electric lights, and constant motion provided a stark contrast to kerosene lamps and quiet foot paths of Kanweaken.

That first week raced by in a blur as Joseph and his family created their new routines. The young teenagers adapted quickly, as teenagers do. They learned to navigate the busy streets, cross at proper corners, and bargain with the market women who chuckled at their astonishment when they were told the prices of certain commodities. Augustus discovered a bookstore and spent hours browsing its shelves. Clara befriended the neighbors' daughter, and the two became inseparable.

Hard Time had been living with Florence on the outskirts of the capital, and she was eager to come to the capital and share city life with her parents and teenage siblings in that crowded, busy apartment. Joseph recognized in her the same drive to learn and adapt that he had always felt.

There was a time when the other children got caught up in a "He said, she said" argument, while she was in another room quietly reading a book. When her name came up, Joseph said, "I know my daughter Hard Time. She doesn't have anything to do with this idle gossip."

Fig. 5 – Raymond, Augustus, Joseph Jr.

In those early days of city life, Mabel discovered the quickest routes to the market, the water pump, and the other places that would define their new daily rhythms. With an ability to create order from chaos that never failed to impress Joseph, she established routines, organized the cramped spaces, and trained the children in their new duties.

But Joseph could see the city was wearing on her. When she spoke of returning to Kanweaken, he understood. She had helped establish this new household, had ensured the children knew how to manage, but the city would never be her home.

Mabel's departure was heartbreaking for her youngest daughter, but she put on a brave face. The morning she left, all the children gathered to say goodbye. Joseph watched as she hugged each one of them, whispering instructions and blessings.

After Mabel left—the only one of his wives who had come to establish the household in Monrovia—Joseph found a house better suited to the family's size. In addition to the six children living in the house with him, friends and relatives were always around.

He watched his children claim their spaces in the house and settle into new daily rhythms. His salary as a representative had made possible this home in the heart of the capital, these opportunities for his children. Yet the very position that provided these advantages also kept him away from them, often late into the evening as congressional sessions stretched on.

The city held its own temptations, as it always had for Joseph. Women were drawn to him here just as they had been in Kanweaken. His presence in a room was somehow magnetic, and it didn't hurt that he was always so meticulous about his appearance. Now, his position in government brought even more attention.

If he had a lady friend at the time, he was very discreet about it. I wouldn't have been surprised if he did. He was Joseph Geleplay, after all.

Joseph bought a parcel of land in Corner West near Popo Beach in New Kru Town and had a large house built for the family, which now included his sixth wife, Louise. The "Big House," as the children called it, had five bedrooms, two bathrooms, a large living room, a dining room, and a kitchen that one of the children declared was large enough to feed half the village back home. The bedrooms could each fit three full beds. Both the front and back porches were generous.

Next to the main house, Joseph built a smaller two-room house with a grocery store attached. This store was stocked and staffed by Hard Time at fourteen years old–a responsibility she took seriously and carried out with pride.

When Hard Time was elected student council president in ninth grade—the first girl in the family to reach that level of education without having children—Joseph's pride knew no bounds. He made it a point to attend every parent-teacher conference, dressed, as always, as if he were going to meet the president himself.

The other children excelled with all of the new opportunities available to them as well. Augustus in particular showed remarkable promise. The boy seemed to absorb knowledge like a sponge. Joseph decided to invest in a private school education for Augustus, seeing in him an exceptional mind that deserved every possible advantage. The investment proved worthwhile, and Augustus developed not only academically but artistically. His ability to capture the essence of his subjects in his drawings was uncanny, and he expressed himself movingly in poetry.

Whatever had happened in the capitol during the day, Joseph could always look forward to coming home to a house vibrating with the energy of his ambitious teenagers. Their voices would carry from different rooms—Augustus either socializing or studying, everyone studying and doing homework first, and infectious laughter erupting from some private joke shared between siblings. The sandy yard would still hold the day's footprints from impromptu games and gatherings.

Even at this hour, the house felt alive with possibility. These children who had once sat on his porch in Kanweaken learning their letters were now dreaming of universities, of careers, of futures that would have seemed impossible just a generation ago. They moved through the Big House with the easy confidence of young people who believed anything was possible. And why shouldn't they? Their father sat in Congress, they had a big and comfortable home in New Kru Town, and every day brought new opportunities to learn and grow.

Joseph would pause sometimes in the doorway, taking in the scene. The homework spread across tables, the proud reports handed to him, the endless projects and plans his children were always hatching. The house itself seemed to embrace their ambitions, its generous rooms offering space for every dream to unfold. Hard Time's careful management of the store next door reflected their shared belief that with enough dedication, any goal could be achieved.

These evening moments reminded Joseph of everything he had worked for—not just the physical structure of this beautiful home but the spirit of possibility it contained. His children were reaching for heights he had once only imagined, and he could see in their bright faces the future he had always envisioned for his people.

Each morning as he dressed for Congress, Joseph paid careful attention to every detail of his appearance. His suits were precisely pressed, his shoes gleaming. Hard Time often stood in his doorway, offering opinions on which suit best suited the day's events. "Not the blue one, Papa; wear the brown. They'll take you more seriously," she would say. He was proud of how fluent she had become in this subtle language of impressions and influence. He wondered whether she was born to it, as he had been, or simply following his example.

As Joseph watched his children helping one another with homework, sharing stories from their respective schools, debating ideas they'd learned in class, it reminded him of his own hunger for knowledge as a young man, now multiplied across all these young minds.

He reflected on how far they'd all come from the gathering of youngsters on his front porch in Kanweaken, each with their own handheld slate and piece of chalk. Before that, when he was a child himself, he had first taught his younger siblings and cousins using whatever materials he could find. Now his own children sat in proper classrooms, with proper books and proper teachers.

"Stay in school," he would tease them. "You don't want to be sitting at home hungry, thinking about how good your neighbor's dinner smells." But this generation needed little encouragement to take advantage of the opportunities life in Monrovia offered them.

These children, this house, this moment in time—it all felt so full of potential. When he stood at the front window in the evenings, watching the city's lights flicker on one by one, Joseph silently breathed a prayer of hope.

12 | JJG

A STATESMAN FOR HIS PEOPLE

Sunlight streamed through the capitol's tall windows as Joseph Juty Geleplay took his place among Liberia's legislators. The year 1976 stretched before him—a year that would test everything he had learned about leadership since those first days of teaching at the missionary school.

While he waited to take his oath, his mind worked through the initiatives he was eager to champion expanded funding for rural schools, improved infrastructure, road connectivity, and development that would reach beyond Monrovia into the heart of the nation. He also would negotiate township status for Kanweaken.

President Tolbert sat in the gallery, the gold chain of office gleaming against his dark suit. His steady gaze moved across the chamber, seeming to assess each new legislator in turn. In the days leading up to the swearing in, a whirlwind of introductions at dinners and meetings, Joseph had been observing the power dynamics at play—the alliances and tensions that shaped Liberian politics. Though Tolbert spoke of unity, the reality was more complex. Joseph knew his effectiveness as one of the nation's few indigenous statesmen would depend on his ability to build bridges while remaining true to his people's interests.

"I do solemnly swear that I will support, uphold, protect and defend the Constitution and laws of the Republic of Liberia, bear true faith and allegiance to the Republic, and will faithfully, conscientiously, and impartially discharge the duties and functions of the office of Representative to the best of my ability, so help me God."

Joseph spoke the oath with measured clarity, each word underlaid with purpose. The path that had led him here—from student to teacher to congressman—had taught him the power of patience and persistence. The same skills that had helped him transform opposition into support in Kanweaken would serve him now.

Yet even as he embraced this new role, Joseph remained acutely aware of the storms that gathered. The price of rice, the main staple of the nation's diet, continued to rise—and discontent within the cities rose along with it. Meanwhile, back at home, farmers without a way to transport their crops across the untamed jungle had few options for providing for their families' basic needs. Without roads and bridges connecting villages to towns, abundance in one region couldn't offset scarcity in another. New infrastructure, Joseph knew, would be critical.

His constituents needed more than the promises that came so easily during campaign speeches and debates. They needed real progress, and they needed it now. He had spent his life building schools and teaching children in Kanweaken, Tiehnpo, and Feloken. He had traded his classroom for Congress, but the essential work remained the same: opening doors for the next generation.

Joseph had already seen how successfully developed towns closer to the capital put their tax revenues to work, and he envisioned that kind of prosperity for Kanweaken. He had known since his early teaching days that government funding was supposedly available for hinterland schools. But he had also seen how rarely that money made it past Monrovia's bureaucracy, disappearing into a maze of corruption and administrative inefficiency.

Township status for Kanweaken would change that equation. The road to Harper gave them an advantage, since goods and people already moved through the village regularly. This created natural opportunities for commerce and development. But Joseph knew the road alone wasn't enough. He needed to convince his fellow legislators that Kanweaken had the potential to become a hub of educational progress for the entire region.

In committee meetings and private conversations, Joseph methodically built his case. He spoke of the young people who had to leave their families behind after eighth grade if they wanted to continue their education. He detailed how a high school would serve not just Kanweaken but also the surrounding villages. When skeptics questioned whether qualified teachers could be found, he drew on his decades of experience as an educator and described practical strategies to train new teachers without them having to leave home.

Finally, an initiative was drafted, and then signed. Getting the paperwork done wasn't the hard part. The real challenge was ensuring the promised resources would actually reach Kanweaken. Joseph had seen too many well-intentioned programs falter in implementation.

To make sure Kanweaken would realize the fruits of all his work, he built relationships with key administrators in Monrovia, creating accountability for the flow of funds. He invited tribal elders to Monrovia and introduced them to these administrators to keep everything transparent. Kanweaken's people would know exactly what was allocated to them, so there would be no way for funds to get misplaced along the way.

His experience straddling traditional and modern systems proved invaluable. When some elders expressed concern about how township status might affect traditional governance structures, Joseph helped broker compromises that respected both systems. He understood that the high school's success would depend on community buy-in as much as government support.

Next came the hard work of turning paper promises into brick-and-mortar reality. Joseph personally made sure construction materials arrived, teachers were hired and paid, and systems were put in place to maintain the school for years to come.

The high school's impact rippled through the community. Families who had resigned themselves to sending teenagers away to Harper or Monrovia could now keep their children close. Young people could imagine futures that didn't require choosing between education and home, and farms began to thrive again with their help.

For Joseph, going back home for visits and seeing students fill those new classrooms validated every hour spent navigating congressional politics and bureaucratic obstacles. Kanweaken's children finally had the same opportunities he had dreamed of decades ago when he first dared to teach against the elders' wishes.

13 | 🏛️JG

THE COUP

Hard Time was spending time with her high school friend Martha Bailey somewhere in Senkor in a nice apartment she shared with her sister Janice. It might have been a birthday, a holiday, or just a random weekend. The details have blurred over time; but what lingered was the laughter that filled the air. No matter what the conversation was, the girls felt safe.

They woke up the morning of April 12, 1980, to the sound of shooting, and they didn't know what to make of it. They later learned from the radio that the executive mansion had been seized, and President Tolbert assassinated. A man none of us had heard of before, Master Sergeant Samuel Kanyon Doe, was the new head of state.

In Corner West, Joseph and the rest of his family also woke to the sounds of gunfire. With shock, he realized that these were not the distant shots of hunters. When he got up and looked out the window, he saw empty streets in the gray, predawn light. He wasn't back home in Kanweaken; he was still in Monrovia. A second concentrated burst rang out—most certainly from an automatic weapon. His first thought was of his children and their future.

He had seen the signs of unrest building during his four years in Congress. Tolbert's promises of change hadn't amounted to much, and people were growing increasingly dissatisfied with the status quo. The attitudes and practices among the political elites had not changed, even within the administration and among the people who worked with Tolbert every day.

Joseph had endured it when his colleagues praised his "exceptional" intelligence and capabilities, as if these traits were anomalies among his people rather than qualities suppressed by generations of systemic exclusion. In meetings, they would gesture to his presence as evidence of progress while continuing to concentrate real power within their Americo-Liberian circles.

He had watched promising legislation languish in committees, had seen resources meant for the hinterland diverted to Monrovia's elite. President Tolbert had campaigned on ending such practices, but the nepotism had only grown more brazen.

Government positions, educational opportunities, and development funds still flowed almost exclusively to Congo people and their families.

The signs of coming violence had been there, though few believed it would really come to this. Street corners had become places of heated debate, where young men would gather to rail against the government. "In the cause of the people, the struggle continues!" they would shout, fists raised. The phrase echoed through the markets and schoolyards.

Progressive Alliance of Liberia activists had been arrested for distributing "seditious" pamphlets. The rice riots of 1979 had shown how quickly frustration could ignite into violence. More indigenous soldiers were joining the army ranks, men who had grown up watching their families labor while Congo people's children went abroad to study.

Still, people had grown accustomed to the threatening slogans painted on walls, the whispered plots, the occasional rally dispersed by police. They had seen it all before—the grumbling, the promises of revolution that never came. The Congo people's grip on power seemed too entrenched, their control of the military too complete, for real change to come through violence. Even those who spoke of revolution seemed to be playing familiar roles in a performance everyone knew would end in compromise or quiet suppression.

Through it all, Joseph had believed in working within the system, in making gradual changes through educating people, just as he had done in the hinterland. Now, the crack of gunfire told him that time for such gradual change had run out.

The radio brought fragments of news throughout the day. President Tolbert was dead, killed in his bed in the executive mansion. Noncommissioned officers of the Armed Forces of Liberia had taken control. Joseph knew that anyone associated with Tolbert's government could be next.

His children looked to him for reassurance, but for the first time in his life, Joseph had no lesson to teach, no story to tell that could make sense of this moment. He could only wait, keeping his family close, listening to the sounds of a city descending into chaos. A curfew was imposed, and all borders were closed.

The Geleplay family rarely left the house, and when they did, they were always in well before curfew. When Joseph went out, he dressed much more simply than he had before. The smart suits that had marked his position as a representative stayed in the closet. He advised his children not to draw attention to themselves in any way when they went out.

Through the windows, he watched once crowded neighborhoods drained and empty. The city that had represented progress, however imperfect, was contracting as everyone retreated into their own private spaces in fear. The market women who had once filled the streets were now understandably staying inside, hoarding the rice and basics they had for their families. At night, the sounds of violence would pierce the darkness—gunfire, screaming, the heavy boots of soldiers enforcing curfew.

One night, the family huddled together as a young woman's cries echoed from nearby—pleas for mercy as she was assaulted by soldiers who had caught her out after curfew. Joseph stood at the window, his hands clenched at his sides, helplessness burning in his chest. He who had always acted to protect others could do nothing but stand in silence as brutality ruled the streets.

His children looked to him for explanations, but how could he explain what he himself struggled to understand? He had seen the corruption and watched resources meant for development disappear into private pockets. But he had continued to believe in the power of education and gradual change—the same path that had transformed Kanweaken and other villages. Now that path seemed to lead nowhere.

In the mornings, rumors would circulate about who had been taken in the night. Any connection to Tolbert's government, any perceived slight to the new military authorities, could bring soldiers to one's door. Joseph knew that all it would take was one person with a grudge, one false accusation about the land disputes back in Kanweaken, and his family's sanctuary could shatter.

He had always taught his children to speak truth to power, but now he counseled caution, watching his proud, highly esteemed, and outspoken children learn to move quietly, to keep their eyes down. "Just be careful," he would tell them, the words feeling insufficient as they left his mouth. "Don't miss curfew."

His life's work had been building bridges between the old ways and the new, between village and city, between Greabo wisdom and Western education. Now those bridges seemed to be burning, and he could only try to keep his family safe amid the flames.

These dark changes rippled outward from Monrovia. News trickled in of unrest in the counties, of old grievances finding violent expression. Joseph thought of his lands in Kanweaken, of the home his wives and children shared, their farms, and the school that had been built on his land. Would they survive? The soldiers proclaiming themselves liberators had no interest in the patient work of building understanding between peoples.

He had taught generations of students to believe in their power to shape Liberia's future through education and civic engagement. Now those same students watched military trucks roll through the streets, watched educated men and women disappear into custody. Some of the young soldiers, he noticed with a pang, were no older than his own students had been when he had filled their heads with facts about the world around them and their hearts with hope.

In the relative safety of his home, Joseph tried to maintain daily routines. He would sit with his children in the living room and talk with them about the news and the mounting uncertainties. They also talked about the past. Memories of silly moments sparked peals of laughter. The family found solace in the stories and jokes they shared, and surviving those dark days strengthened their bonds.

Prices skyrocketed and basic needs grew scarce. There were some things that were almost impossible to get even if one had the money. Nevertheless, Joseph made sure there was always food in the house—his experience managing resources served his family well as the situation became more strained.

But there were changes he couldn't shield them from. The sound of cars approaching would bring sudden silence to conversations. A knock at the door could freeze the breath in their lungs. Joseph found himself watching his children develop new instincts as they became more guarded and closed. They were learning lessons he had never wanted to teach them.

The Congo people had held power so long they had forgotten it could be taken from them. Joseph wondered if the soldiers now patrolling the streets, drunk on their sudden authority, would learn the same lesson. Would the oppressed become the oppressor? When would the cycle end? He wondered whether some divides ran too deep to heal.

Markets eventually reopened, though less abundant than before. People ventured out earlier in the mornings and later in the evenings, testing the boundaries of curfew. But the sound of military trucks still silenced conversations, and disappearances continued. The new government spoke of equal rights while wielding power with the same brutal efficiency they had condemned in their predecessors.

Joseph watched his colleagues navigate this changed landscape—some rushing to curry favor with the new authorities, others withdrawing into careful silence. He thought of his own years of careful bridge-building, accomplishing what he could within the system. Perhaps it was time to step away, to return to the work he knew best.

One evening, after his family had gone to bed, Joseph imagined a silhouette of the capitol building—still standing but completely dark where lights used to shine out from the windows of familiar offices and halls when colleagues worked late. His mind returned to Kanweaken, to the school he had built there, to the farms and the familiar rhythms of village life. His children needed stability now, not the constant tension of wondering who might be taken next.

His mind was restless as always, mapping out contingencies against an unpredictable future. The military government was not hurrying to return to civilian rule, and the idea of staying in Monrovia felt more like sinking. He needed a new beginning.

Kanweaken called Joseph, and he decided to return home. The memories of the simplicity of life there painted a stark contrast to the tension of the city living under a volatile regime with an uncertain future. The thought of returning to the place that had shaped him was both comforting and bittersweet.

Joseph looked around one last time at the high ceilings, the polished floors that had witnessed so many family gatherings. Everything they had built here felt provisional now, temporary in a way the mud-brick walls of Kanweaken never had.

As much as Joseph wanted to take his entire family back to Kanweaken, most of his children were adults now. They had formed meaningful relationships in Monrovia and did not want to go back to the interior with its slow-paced lifestyle, so far removed from the opportunities of the modern world. Joseph respected their choices, even as it pained him to imagine leaving without them, but he was confident that the values he had instilled were strong enough to keep them grounded.

Joseph's family, including Joan and her children, stayed in Monrovia. The Big House was never empty, as other family members continued to come and go. It was always the first and last stop when relatives visited or moved to Monrovia and when they left. There was never a day the doors were locked.

Those days weren't untouched by the chaos going on throughout the city, but there was still a rhythm to them. Beyond survival, there was a simple joy. The front porch was where everyone hung out at the end of the day, listening to one another's stories, though in those days those stories were sometimes painful and humiliating. And so life in Monrovia continued day by day, with Joseph's family managing whatever they could and finding strength in the simple act of togetherness.

14 | FINAL RETURN

T he familiar scent of wood smoke and Mabel's
cooking drew Joseph home as soon as he
stepped out of the car. His wives and children had
kept the garden thriving while he made his new home
in the capitol. The cassava patches were thick with
greenery as always, pineapples ripening in neat rows.
Inside, the rooms filled quickly with the voices of his
family reuniting, grandchildren darting between the
women's *lappa*, everyone talking at once about what
had happened, what would be different now.

Kanweaken was home, but it was no longer his
only home. His thoughts drifted to his children in the
Big House. Even with the government in chaos,
Joseph saw work still to be done in Monrovia. People
still needed laws and protection. A new order would
need to be established, and perhaps something good
could emerge from these changes.

Here in town, the air crackled with a new energy. Joseph felt it first at the market area when one of the senior elders stopped him. The old man's smile didn't reach his eyes. "Teacher Joe," he said, using Joseph's old title like a weapon. "We hear you ran from Monrovia when the soldiers came for the Congo people."

"My family is as safe there as they are here," Joseph replied evenly. "I'm here to visit and take care of business."

"Safe?" The elder's sarcastic laugh drew others closer. "Maybe you're not all that safe here."

Joseph drew in a sharp breath.

"Now is when we take back what's ours. That land you tricked from us with that Congo paper—you knew the road was coming, didn't you? You knew what the land would be worth."

Joseph kept his voice steady. "I bought that land fairly, as our customs require. The deed just made it legal under national law."

"National law?" Another man joined in. "Congo law, you mean. Those laws are finished now. The warriors in Monrovia showed us that." A murmur of approval went through the gathering crowd.

Joseph looked at faces he had known for decades—men whose children he had taught and fed. They looked back at him as if he were a stranger, as if the coup had erased not just Congo rule but all of the personal history between them.

The elder turned to the crowd and said, "The land Joseph Geleplay took belongs to the people!" Then lowering his voice so only Joseph could hear he said with a menacing smile, "We'll put it right again."

Joseph mingled a little and walked back to the family home, feeling the stares of old neighbors and family friends boring into his back.

He was back in Monrovia two weeks later when the letter arrived. The elders now claimed they had been "innocent" of his owning the five hundred acres, that everything he had done regarding the land had been done in secret. They gave him one month to surrender his deed.

Joseph's head began to throb as he read. By the time he had read the letter through three times and set it down, his hands were shaking. The signatures at the bottom were elders who had watched him grow up and overseen nearly every major decision in his life.

They had said "no" and later "yes" when he wanted to go and study with those first missionaries who came to Kanweaken—Philip and Grace Elsea. They had driven him out of town for teaching their children, and then when his teaching brought prestige to his new home in Tiehnpo, they devised a trick to bring him back. They had sabotaged his first and second run for Congress, then given their blessing for his third campaign. These men had witnessed and approved his original purchase of the land, and now they were trying to take it away.

These men who had helped shape the life of Joseph Geleplay, from his earliest days, now wrote as if he had deceived them, as if the legal deed he obtained from President Tubman himself was worthless. The formal language of the letter, with its carbon copies to officials, showed how thoroughly the coup had changed things. The old power structures were being dismantled—not in service of justice, but only to settle old scores.

Joseph unfolded the two pages and read them again. His eyes kept returning to that single line typed in capital letters: IN THE CAUSE OF THE PEOPLE! THE STRUGGLE CONTINUES.

The words were like a bitter joke. What "people" did they mean? Not the children who studied in the school he helped build. Not the farmers whose rights he had defended against the mining companies. Not the families who came to him for help with their own land disputes. No, "the people" in this letter meant only those who saw their chance to take what they wanted in the chaos of the coup.

One acre. They would "allow" him one acre of his own land. The land he had bought fairly, the land where he had planted gardens and built houses for his family, the land he had protected from foreign mining interests. They wanted to take it all except for one acre.

He noted the deadline: November 28, 1980. One month. Joseph reached for a clean sheet of paper and began writing a letter to Arthur Williams, a lawyer who had been recommended to him when he was working to secure township status for Kanweaken. A few hours later, Joseph's letter to Counsellor Williams was ready:

Dear Counsellor Williams,

I am here to bring my grievances to your knowledge
and honestly request your kind intervention legally and
to act as my legal counsel in a case before me about
land and properties owned in sixty lots.

Before narrating the whole detail of this matter to you,
I would like to acquaint you of my citizenship of the
tribe of Gbeapo. My parents are natives of Gbeapo tribe
and were born in Kanweaken town, Gbeapo District #2,
Grand Gedeh county, R. L. I was born May 20, 1919,
and now am 61 years and 8 months old. I am a father
of twenty-six living children, thirty living
grandchildren, and five great-grandchildren.

I started schooling in 1930, and I was able to complete
the eighth grade. I then applied for a teaching job in an
Assembly of God Missions school and was successful. I
then started teaching in my hometown, Kanweaken. I
taught for six years without pay. Because of the love of
my people, I never bothered about it, not even to the
missionaries. Until in 1950, through the help of the late
President William V. S. Tubman, I started receiving an
amount of thirty dollars per month. After I finished
high school, I was paid fifty dollars per month. Looking
at the conditions of how things were, I then deemed it
wise to negotiate for a farmland from my own people,
which I did by asking for a five-hundred-acre parcel on

the side of the road leading from Cape Palmas to Tiehnpo and passing through our town, Kanweaken. The elders of the town and some of the citizens of the town were present when my request was granted. I was charged an amount of thirty dollars cash, six large bottles of cane juice, and ten heads of tobacco, which I paid and was awarded a tribal certificate by the same elders. That was in 1962. At the time none of us ever dreamt that streets would pass through our town.

I was also a public-school teacher. In the same year, two of my friends that bought their land together from the elders in the same town had joined me to send for a government surveyor. So, we sent for Mr. Power Freeman from Monrovia to conduct the land survey. We paid his fare to and from and services rendered. I paid him $275.00 with the exception of food while he was in Kanweaken.

I then told Mr. Freeman to prepare for me two certificates, one for thirteen acres where I decided to erect my houses and the balance for live trees. The thirteen-acres deed was signed by the late President W.V.S. Tubman.

Lastly, when I carried my tribal certificate to late president William R. Tolbert, Jr., he told me to change the first deed because it did not bear his signature but that of Tubman. So, I took it back to Mr. Freeman to change the deed to William R. Tolbert's signature, which he did, and President Tolbert signed it in 1976 when I bought my land before the township of Kanweaken came to be.

Lastly, the township commissioner, Mr. George Nagbe and some citizens of our town Kanweaken sent me a letter in October 1980, requesting me to send them my documents pertaining to my land and properties so they could destroy them because my land is located in the heart of the township. So I went with my tribal certificate and a photocopy of my deed. They took the tribal certificate and compelled me to sign a promissory note they prepared stating that if I didn't give them my original deeds, they would sue me to any higher authority in Liberia. For security reasons, I did sign the same, but what I prepared is what they refused to sign.

Knowing that I'll come to the government to seek refuge, I therefore come to you as my counsellor for redress.

Yours truly,

Joseph J. Geleplay

"They've appealed again," Arthur said, spreading the latest court documents across his desk. "Third time now."

Joseph nodded, unsurprised. Through the office window, he could see the streets of Monrovia bustling with its usual activity, as if the coup had changed nothing at all. "Then we'll present our case again."

"The same evidence. The same witnesses. The same result." Arthur's frustration was evident in his voice. "They're just trying to wear you down."

"No," Joseph said quietly. "They're afraid. When people are afraid, they fight against change even when change would help them. But look—" He picked up one of the court documents. "These appeals, they're following the legal process now. They're learning there are ways to resolve conflicts without violence. That's progress."

Arthur stared at him. "Progress? They're trying to take your land!"

"And we're showing them how to fight with words and laws instead of violence." Joseph smiled. "The next generation will remember this. They'll see there are better ways than force. We must not give up."

Arthur leaned back in his chair, studying his old friend. Joseph had lost weight in recent months, and new lines creased his face, but his eyes still held that familiar spark of determination.

"You're a better man than I am, Joe," Arthur said finally. "If someone kept dragging me back to court over land I'd bought fair and square..."

"What else can we do?" Joseph spread his hands. "Hold grudges? Let anger eat us up inside? No."

He stood and walked to the window. "My people are finding their voice. They're learning to read contracts, file appeals, speak up in court. This is progress! Even if they're using these things against me now, they're still learning. The skills will serve them well in the future."

Arthur sorted through the papers, selecting the ones that needed signatures. "Your optimism is going to bankrupt you, you know that?" But there was admiration in his voice. He had watched Joseph work tirelessly for his people while in Congress. Even now, facing betrayal from his own people, he was thinking about their future.

"Not bankruptcy," Joseph said, turning back from the window. "Investment. In twenty years, when someone else tries to take advantage of our people, they'll know how to defend themselves properly. They'll remember these court battles."

He sat down to sign the papers Arthur had drafted for the next hearing, his hand steady and sure. Arthur noticed that even now, Joseph took time to read each document carefully before signing. Always the teacher, always setting an example, even when no one was watching.

Every court battle ended in Joseph's favor—first the local courts, then the county courts, and finally the

Supreme Court itself. Each time the judges examined the documentation and heard testimony about the original purchase, they ruled that the land rightfully belonged to Joseph Juty Geleplay.

But legal victories meant little in a country where order was crumbling. Each time Joseph won, the elders would appeal, dragging the process out longer. The court battles drained his energy and resources, but it wasn't about the money anymore. It was about the truth. He wanted to show his people that there were better ways to resolve conflicts than by force and intimidation.

Then came the summons to return to Kanweaken for a meeting. Joseph knew in his heart what they intended, but he went anyway. Perhaps there was still a chance for understanding, to find a way forward that would heal these wounds between him and his people.

The meeting was held outside of the town in a secluded area in the bush. When he arrived at the site, men he had known all his life sat in stony silence as he was called to the front. Joseph's eyes widened as a document was given to him. "You tricked us; you knew the value of the land, and you stole it from under our noses." They wanted him to sign away his rights to the land. When he tried to speak about the court decisions, about how he had developed the land to benefit everyone, about his plans for a school, they cut him off.

"Sign," they said, "or you won't leave this place."

The pen shook in Joseph's hand. After everything, this was what it had come to. Raw power exercising its will. The same thing he had spent his life fighting against, now wielded by his own people.

He signed.

The car ride back to Monrovia seemed longer than usual, each bump in the rutted road sending waves of pain through Joseph's body. His shirt was soaked with sweat despite the cool night air. He tried to wave off help getting out of the car, but his legs wouldn't cooperate.

Louise took one look at his flushed face and said, "You're going to the hospital," in a tone that allowed no argument.

The hospital walls were the same pale green they'd always been, but they seemed to shimmer and dance in Joseph's fevered vision. The doctors spoke in low voices about stress and about his heart. He heard them, but his mind was swirling about what had happened.

Joseph had better days and then worse days. Joan went to see him nearly every day. At first, he was able to speak, but within a few days, he lost that ability. Joan mentioned that he wished to write, but his hands were too weak to grasp the pen.

Joseph Juty Geleplay died December 15, 1982, leaving behind twenty-seven children and dozens of grandchildren to carry on his memory and his great spirit. Hard Time was seventeen, spending the Christmas break with her sister Ethel in Yekapa when they told them. She stood in her living room, unable to move, unable to believe what she was hearing. Her father—the man who had trusted her to run a grocery store on her own when everyone else thought she was too young, who had beamed with pride when she became student council president, who had seen such promise in his first wife's youngest daughter—was gone.

All those questions Hard Time had saved up to ask him the next time she saw him would remain forever unasked. When he was around, everything made sense—the world seemed full of possibility, and she felt like she could do anything. He had that effect on people. When he looked at you, really looked at you, you felt precious, like you mattered more than anything else in that moment. No one else ever saw Hard Time quite the way her father did.

Now that clear, steady light was gone from the world. Joseph, who could make anyone feel valued just by the way he listened, who could explain anything to anyone with infinite patience, who saw the best in people even when they betrayed him—he would never again turn that gentle, knowing gaze her way and make everything feel right.

EPILOGUE ||

Over four decades have passed since Joseph drew his last breath. This man was driven by a vision that on the surface seemed simple—a land where people could enjoy the benefits of the modern world while honoring the traditions of their ancestors and stewarding the abundant resources of the land for generations to come. He envisioned a future where education and political representation would secure everyone a rightful place at the table of civic life.

Central to this vision were the five hundred acres of land Joseph bought. He envisioned building schools, libraries, and a hub of learning that would transform Kanweaken from a small village into a center of education and opportunity. Yet, in the decades since his passing, Joseph's visions are rarely spoken of. The land he fought for remains in dispute, caught in an unresolved battle between his descendants and the townspeople.

Meanwhile, the Geleplay family continues to grow. Joseph's children now have their own grandchildren, and even great-great grandchildren.

Our lineage is strong, and our legacy will continue for generations to come.

Though Joseph did not live to see his ultimate vision realized, his impact endured long after his passing. In 1985, when Peace Corps volunteer Richard Bowen arrived to teach mathematics in Kanweaken, he found a town transformed by Joseph's earlier work. The locals spoke often of the teacher-turned-statesman who had elevated their village into a township through his dedication to education and public service. "It was a proud era for Kanweaken," recalled one resident. Joseph was remembered as a figure of deep respect and admiration.

The seeds Joseph planted continued to bear fruit through the decades. When Bowen returned to visit in 2018, he observed how the educational foundation Joseph established had evolved—the school infrastructure had expanded, and more girls were pursuing education, steps toward the inclusive vision Joseph had championed. Though challenges remained, the progress gave testament to the lasting power of Joseph's dream.

Today, Joseph's legacy lives on not only through the physical changes in Kanweaken, but through the changed mindsets of its people. His belief that education could lift up an entire community while preserving its cultural roots proved prescient. While the full scope of his vision remains unrealized, the path he carved continues to guide new generations toward greater opportunity and engagement in civic life. In this way, though Joseph's earthly journey has ended, his life's mission endures through all those who carry forward his dream of a future where tradition and progress walk hand in hand.

Fig. 6 – Commemorations of Joseph's life in Harlem newspaper

Fig. 7 – Joseph's Headstone

ABOUT THE AUTHOR||

Victoria Geleplay Corlon is the daughter of Joseph Juty Geleplay. Originally from Liberia, she now calls Delaware, USA, her home where she lives with her husband and two sons.

As a proud alumna of Wilmington University, she holds a Bachelor of Science in Nursing and has worn many hats throughout her dynamic healthcare career—from Medical-Surgical to Critical Care to the operating room.

Today, she serves as a Psychiatric-Mental Health and Addiction nurse, bringing compassion and insight to one of the most complex frontiers of modern medicine. *Between Two Worlds* is her debut book and a testament to her dedication not just to healing bodies, but to telling powerful stories.

FAMILY TREE

"Joseph Juty Geleplay's Descendents"

(Pages 1-12)

Joseph Juty Geleplay's Descendants

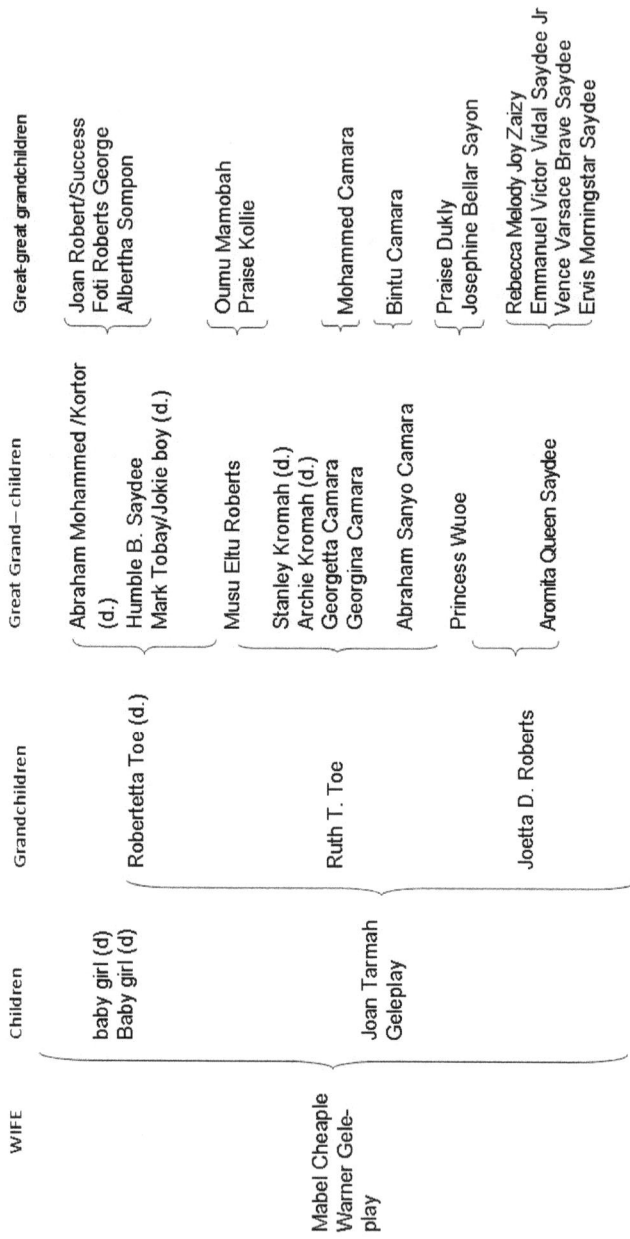

WIFE	Children	Grandchildren	Great Grand—children	Great-great grandchildren
Mabel Cheaple Warner Gele-play	baby girl (d) Baby girl (d)	Robertetta Toe (d.)	Abraham Mohammed /Kortor (d.)	Joan Robert/Success Foti Roberts George Albertha Sompon
			Humble B. Saydee	
			Mark Tobay/Jokie boy (d.)	
			Musu Eltu Roberts	Oumu Mamobah Praise Kollie
	Joan Tarmah Geleplay	Ruth T. Toe	Stanley Kromah (d.) Archie Kromah (d.) Georgetta Camara Georgina Camara	
				Mohammed Camara
			Abraham Sanyo Camara	Bintu Camara
			Princess Wuoe	Praise Dukly Josephine Bellar Sayon
		Joetta D. Roberts	Aromita Queen Saydee	Rebecca Melody Joy Zaizy Emmanuel Victor Vidal Saydee Jr Vence Varsace Brave Saydee Ervis Morningstar Saydee

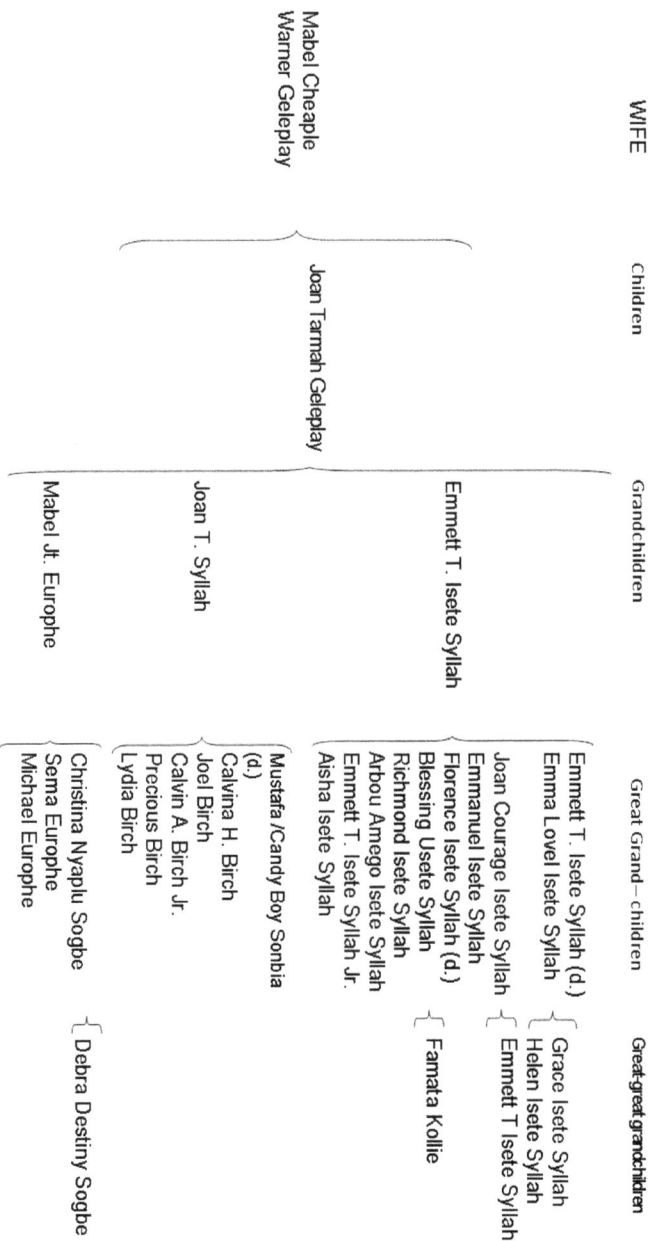

WIFE	Children	Grandchildren	Great Grand–children	Great-great grandchildren
Mabel Cheaple Warner Geleplay	Joan Tarmah Geleplay	Emmett T. Isete Syllah	Emmett T. Isete Syllah (d.)	Grace Isete Syllah / Helen Isete Syllah / Emmett T Isete Syllah
			Emma Lovel Isete Syllah	
			Joan Courage Isete Syllah	
			Emmanuel Isete Syllah	
			Florence Isete Syllah (d.)	
			Blessing Usete Syllah	Famata Kollie
			Richmond Isete Syllah	
			Arbou Amego Isete Syllah	
			Emmett T. Isete Syllah Jr.	
			Aisha Isete Syllah	
		Joan T. Syllah	Mustafa /Candy Boy Sonbia (d.)	
			Calvina H. Birch	
			Joel Birch	
			Calvin A. Birch Jr.	
			Precious Birch	
			Lydia Birch	
		Mabel Jt. Europhe	Christina Nyaplu Sogbe	Debra Destiny Sogbe
			Sema Europhe	
			Michael Europhe	

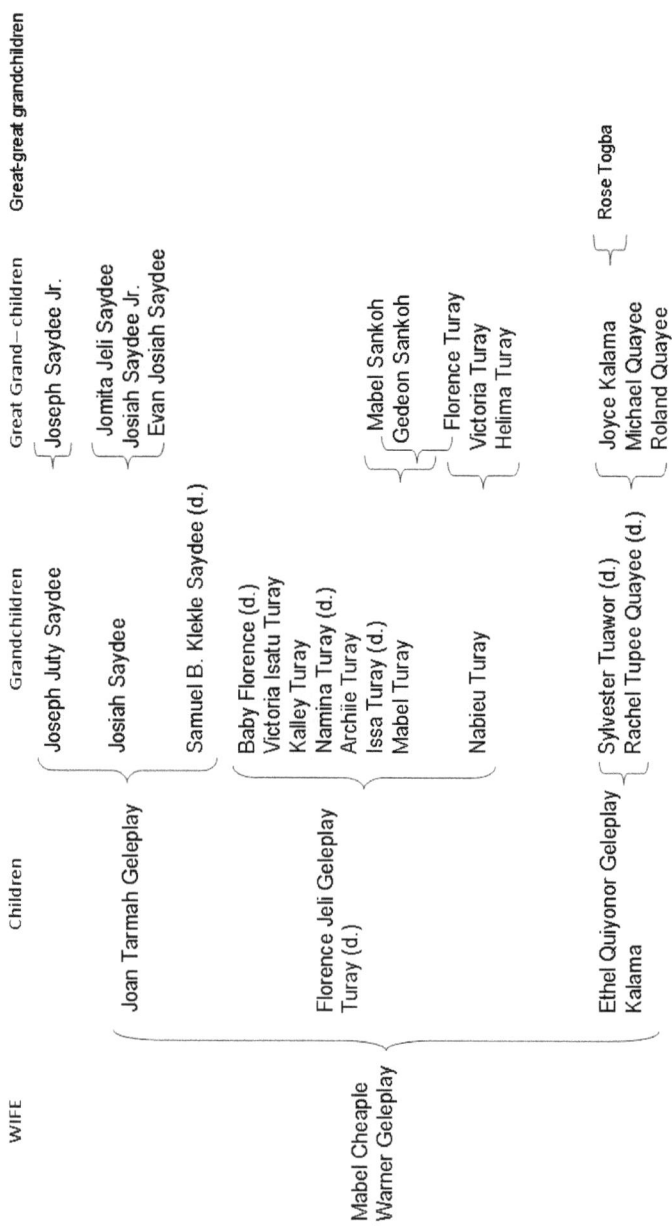

WIFE	Children	Grandchildren	Great Grand—children	Great-great grandchildren
Mabel Cheaple Warner Geleplay	Joan Tarmah Geleplay	Joseph Juty Saydee	Joseph Saydee Jr.	
		Josiah Saydee	Jomita Jeli Saydee Josiah Saydee Jr. Evan Josiah Saydee	
		Samuel B. Klekle Saydee (d.)		
	Florence Jeli Geleplay Turay (d.)	Baby Florence (d.) Victoria Isatu Turay Kalley Turay Namina Turay (d.) Archie Turay Issa Turay (d.) Mabel Turay		
		Nabieu Turay	Mabel Sankoh Gedeon Sankoh Florence Turay Victoria Turay Helima Turay	
	Ethel Quiyonor Geleplay Kalama	Sylvester Tuawor (d.) Rachel Tupee Quayee (d.)	Joyce Kalama Michael Quayee Roland Quayee	Rose Togba

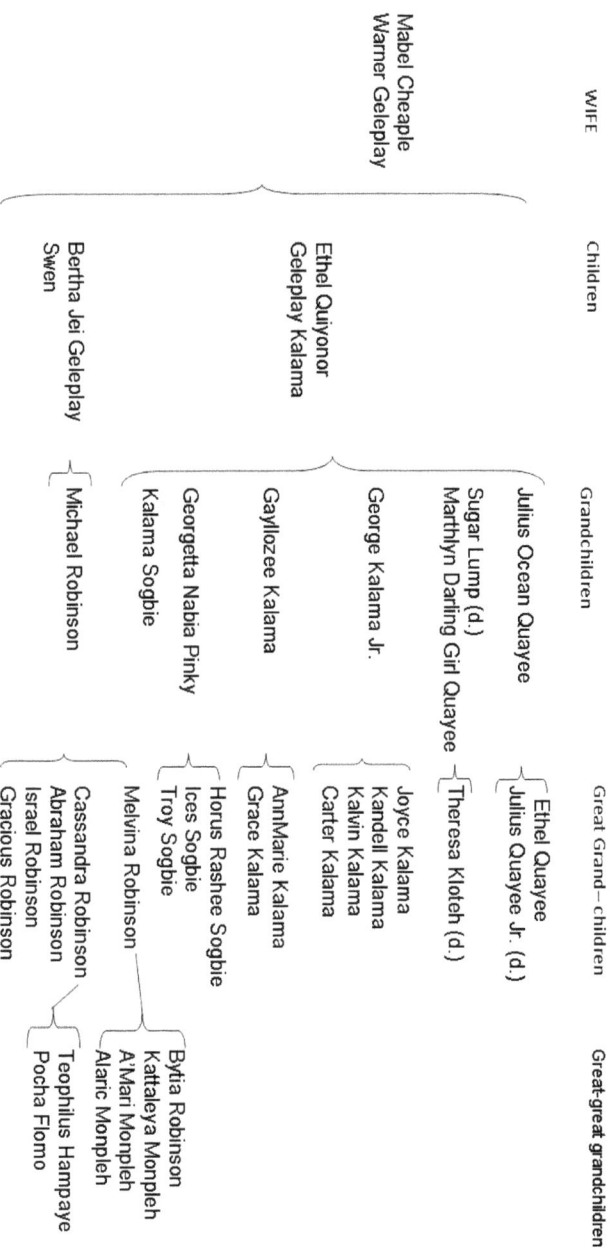

WIFE	Children	Grandchildren	Great Grand–children	Great-great grandchildren
Mabel Cheaple Warner Geleplay	Ethel Quiyonor Geleplay Kalama	Julius Ocean Quayee	Ethel Quayee Julius Quayee Jr. (d.)	
		Sugar Lump (d.)		
		Marthlyn Darling Girl Quayee	Theresa Kloteh (d.)	
		George Kalama Jr.	Joyce Kalama Kandell Kalama Kalvin Kalama Carter Kalama	
		Gayllozee Kalama	AnnMarie Kalama Grace Kalama	
		Georgetta Nabia Pinky	Horus Rashee Sogbie Ices Sogbie Troy Sogbie	
		Kalama Sogbie	Melvina Robinson	Bytia Robinson Kattaleya Monpleh A'Mari Monpleh Alaric Monpleh
	Bertha Jei Geleplay Swen	Michael Robinson	Cassandra Robinson Abraham Robinson Israel Robinson Gracious Robinson	Teophilus Hampaye Pocha Flomo

WIFE	Children	Grandchildren	Great Grand-children	Great-great grand-children
Mabel Cheaple Warner Geleplay	Bertha Jei Geleplay Swen	Jack Nimely	Jemal Nimely Jaden Nimely Jack Nimely III Jennifer Nimely	
		Kelvin Motie Swen	Mekey Nimely Amyni Swen Asanda Swen Asha Swen	
		Jerenifer Nimely Witherspoon	Jerenifer Surprise Witherspoon Jeremy Witherspoon Jenelle Witherspoon	
	Raymond Tidweh Geleplay	Marie Geleplay Victoria Hardtime Geleplay II		
		Mable Cheaple Geleplay II Romel Geleplay Raystina Geleplay Gracious Geleplay	Melvina Garswah baby boy (d.) Kelvin Garswah Destiny Garswah	
	Victoria Tenneh Hardtime Geleplay	Wilfred Sackie G, Corlon Vatekeh Juty Corlon	baby girl (d.) Rachel HT David	

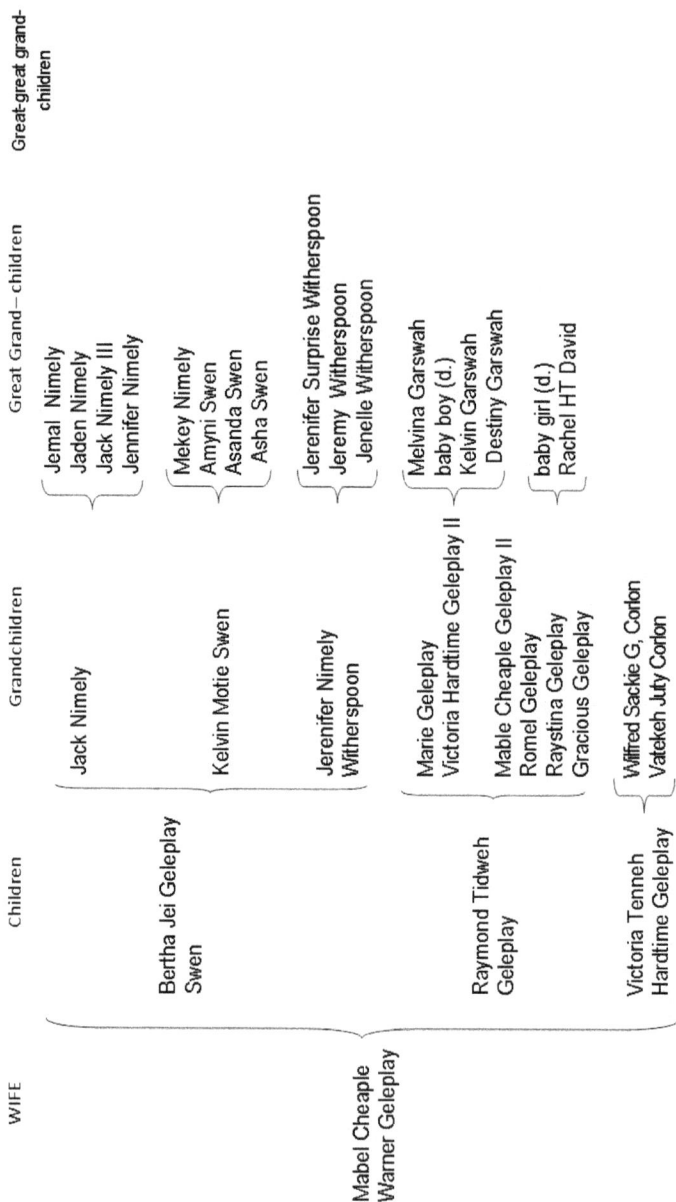

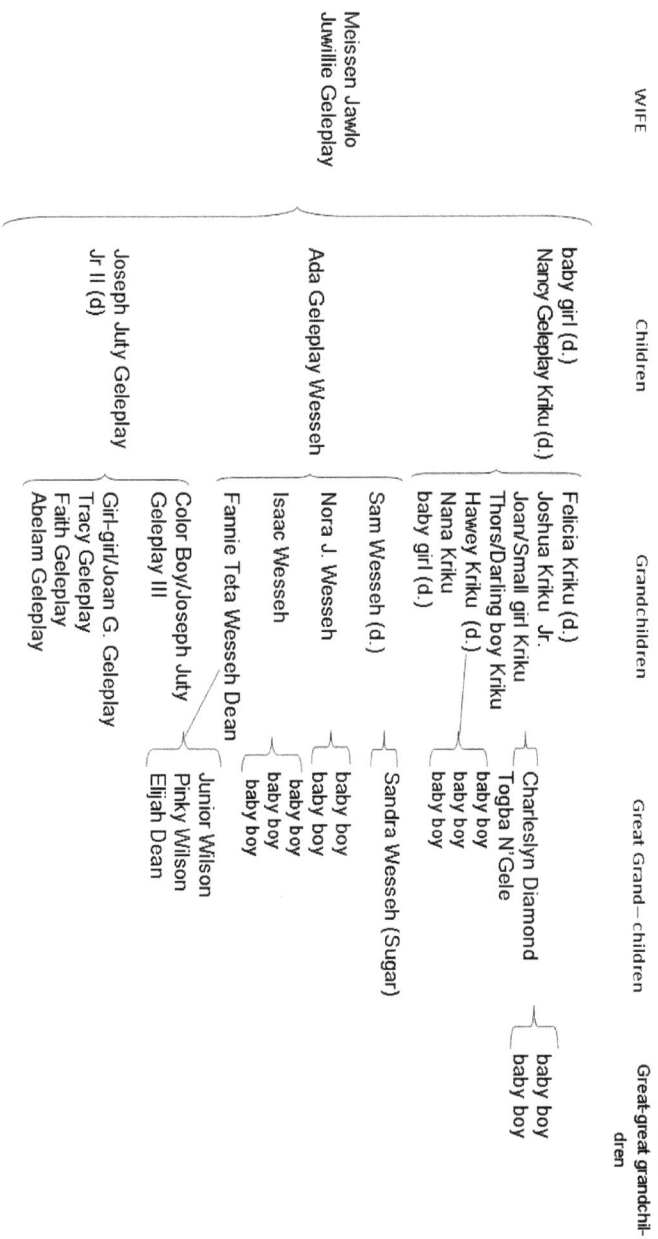

WIFE	Children	Grandchildren	Great Grand–children	Great-great grandchildren
Meissen Jawlo Juwillie Geleplay	baby girl (d.)			
	Nancy Geleplay Kriku (d.)	Felicia Kriku (d.)		
		Joshua Kriku Jr.		
		Joan/Small girl Kriku		
		Thors/Darling boy Kriku		
		Hawey Kriku (d.)	Charleslyn Diamond	baby boy
			Togba N'Gele	baby boy
		Nana Kriku	baby boy	
			baby boy	
			baby boy	
		baby girl (d.)		
	Ada Geleplay Wesseh	Sam Wesseh (d.)	Sandra Wesseh (Sugar)	
		Nora J. Wesseh	baby boy	
			baby boy	
		Isaac Wesseh	baby boy	
			baby boy	
		Fannie Teta Wesseh Dean	Junior Wilson	
			Pinky Wilson	
			Elijah Dean	
		Color Boy/Joseph Juty Geleplay III		
	Joseph Juty Geleplay Jr II (d.)	Girl-girl/Joan G. Geleplay		
		Tracy Geleplay		
		Faith Geleplay		
		Abelam Geleplay		

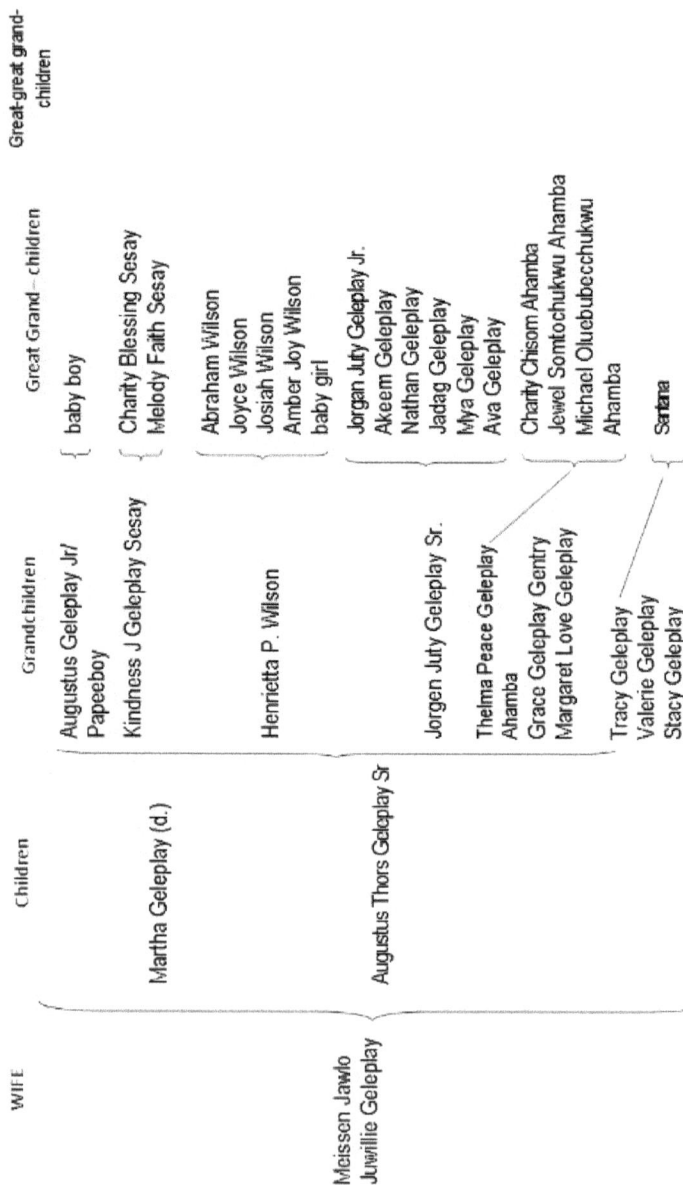

WIFE	Children	Grandchildren	Great Grand—children	Great-great grand-children
Meissen Jawlo Juwillie Geleplay	Martha Geleplay (d.)	Augustus Geleplay Jr/ Papeeboy	baby boy	
		Kindness J Geleplay Sesay	Charity Blessing Sesay Melody Faith Sesay	
		Henrietta P. Wilson	Abraham Wilson Joyce Wilson Josiah Wilson Amber Joy Wilson baby girl	
	Augustus Thors Geleplay Sr	Jorgen Juty Geleplay Sr.	Jorgan Juty Geleplay Jr. Akeem Geleplay Nathan Geleplay Jadag Geleplay Mya Geleplay Ava Geleplay	
		Thelma Peace Geleplay Ahamba	Charity Chisom Ahamba Jewel Somtochukwu Ahamba Michael Oluebubecchukwu Ahamba	
		Grace Geleplay Gentry		
		Margaret Love Geleplay		
		Tracy Geleplay Valerie Geleplay Stacy Geleplay	Santana	

WIFE	Children	Grandchildren	Great Grand–children	Great-great grandchildren
Meissen Jawlo Juwillie Geleplay	Sampson Teacher Geleplay	Cynthia Geleplay	Marthlyn David / Joseph Geleplay / Jerry David / Terry David	
		Precious Geleplay	Peterline D. Dargba / Vester / Betty / Daddy Boy Sieh / Paul Sieh	
		Ethelyne Geleplay / Jeff Geleplay	Mercy	
		Bill/T-boy Geleplay	Mary Geleplay	
		Gitty Geleplay	Pinky Cheap / Joseph S. Torbor	
		Melvina Juah Geleplay	Eva Poka / Favor Poka	
		Baby T Geleplay	Grace	

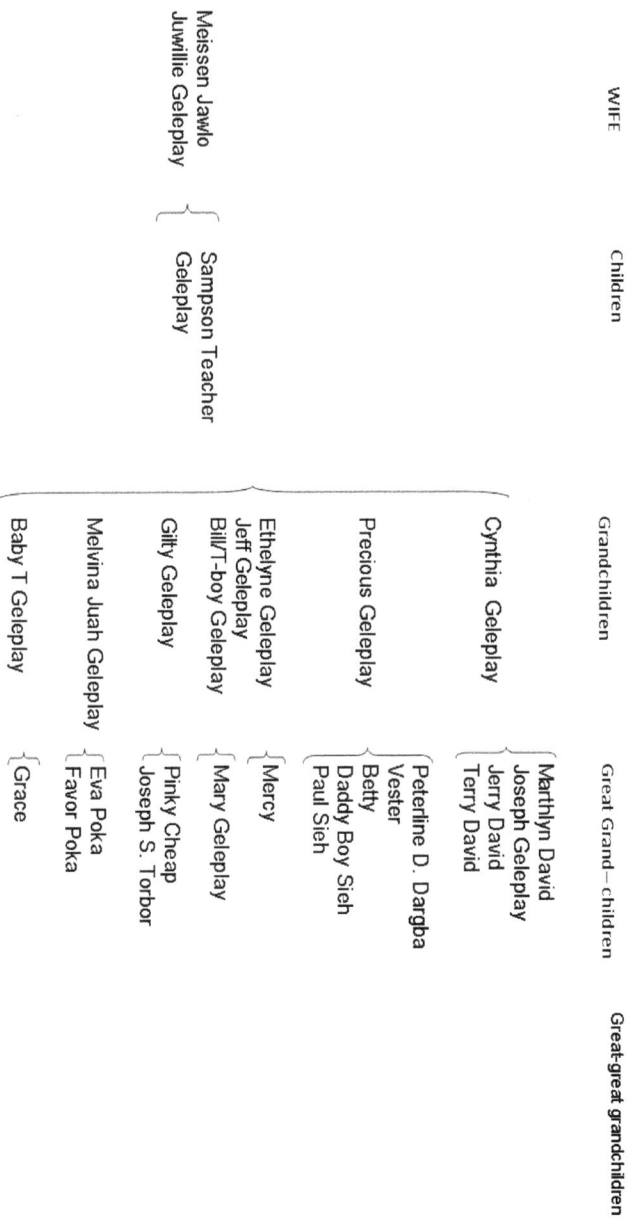

WIFE	Children	Grandchildren	Great Grand–children	Great-great grand-children
Meissen Jawlo Juwillie Geleplay	Sampson Teacher Geleplay	Lovette Geleplay Sonia Geleplay	Rose	
		Agabah Musa Sheriff	Agabah Musa Sheriff Jr. Sekou Bill Sheriff	
		Isaiah W. Tweh	Praise Irene Tweh Angel Tweh(d)	
		Diana D. Doe	Robert Rendy Williams	
		Saydu Taweh Kuyetah		
		Darius Mulbah		
		Mageman Agents Sheriff (d.)		
	Esther T Geleplay			
	Beorah K Geleplay/Dortus	Mageman		
	Martha Geleplay Dargba			
	Martha's twin brother (d.)	Seah		
	Evelyn Geleplay			
Esther Wele Geleplay	Clara Geleplay Cooper	Gibson Gbalah (d) Massa Cooper baby girl (d) Namuyon T Cooper Aquila Bouwoulo Cooper		

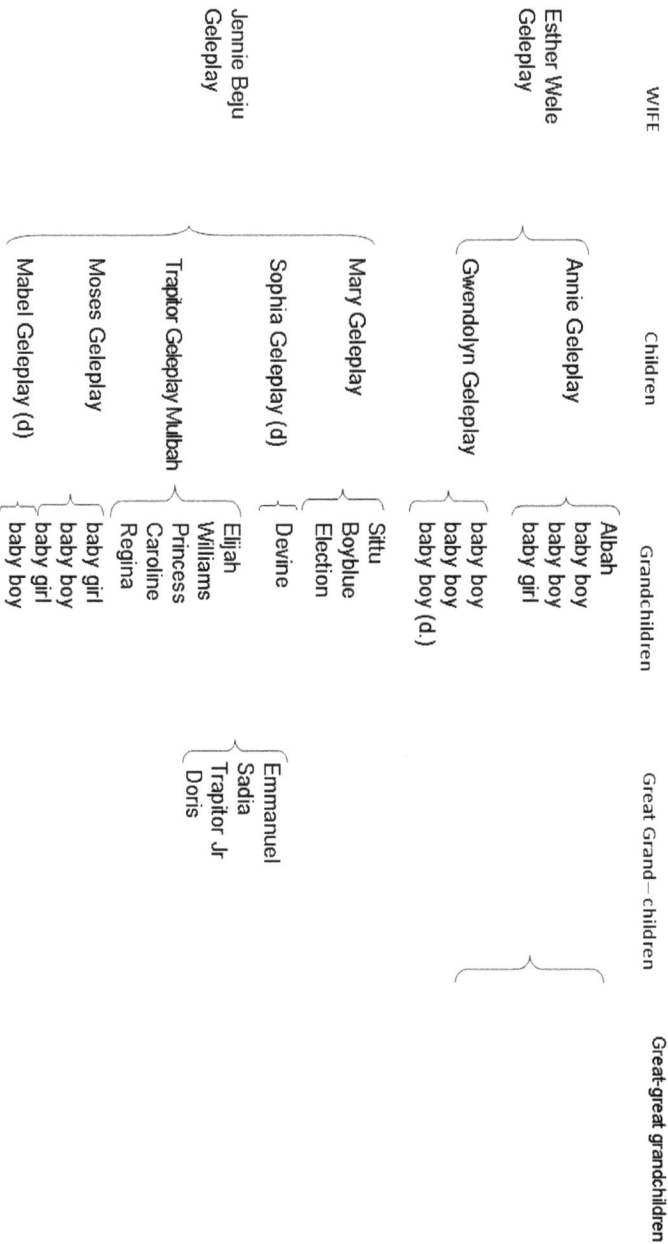

WIFE	Children	Grandchildren	Great Grand–children	Great-great grandchildren
Esther Wele Geleplay	Annie Geleplay	Albah / baby boy / baby boy / baby girl		
	Gwendolyn Geleplay	baby boy / baby boy / baby boy (d.)		
	Mary Geleplay	Sittu / Boyblue / Election		
	Sophia Geleplay (d)	Devine		
Jennie Beju Geleplay	Trapitor Geleplay Mulbah	Elijah / Williams / Princess / Caroline / Regina	Emmanuel / Sadia / Trapitor Jr / Doris	
	Moses Geleplay	baby girl / baby boy / baby girl / baby boy		
	Mabel Geleplay (d)			

- 229 -

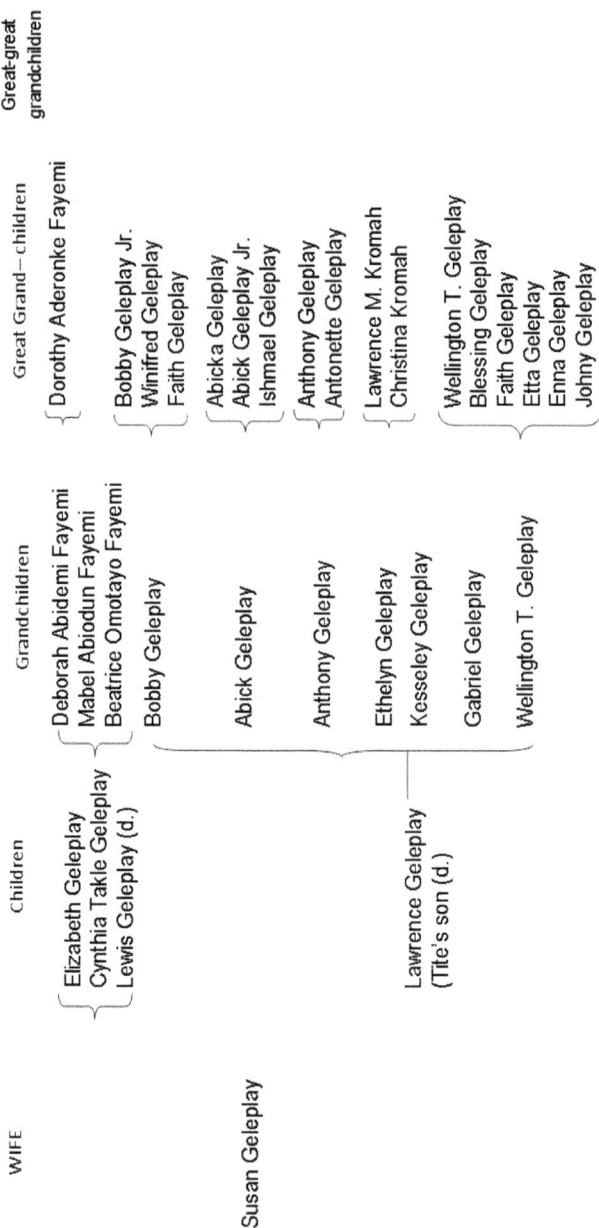

WIFE	Children	Grandchildren	Great Grand–children	Great-great grandchildren
Susan Geleplay	Elizabeth Geleplay Cynthia Takle Geleplay Lewis Geleplay (d.)	Deborah Abidemi Fayemi Mabel Abiodun Fayemi Beatrice Omotayo Fayemi	Dorothy Aderonke Fayemi	
		Bobby Geleplay	Bobby Geleplay Jr. Winifred Geleplay Faith Geleplay	
		Abick Geleplay	Abicka Geleplay Abick Geleplay Jr. Ishmael Geleplay	
		Anthony Geleplay	Anthony Geleplay Antonette Geleplay	
		Ethelyn Geleplay Kesseley Geleplay	Lawrence M. Kromah Christina Kromah	
	Lawrence Geleplay (Tite's son (d.))	Gabriel Geleplay Wellington T. Geleplay	Wellington T. Geleplay Blessing Geleplay Faith Geleplay Etta Geleplay Enna Geleplay Johny Geleplay	

- 230 -

Children	Grandchildren	Great Grand–children	Great-great grand-children
Lawrence Geleplay (Tite's son)(d)	Prince Geleplay	Lawrence Geleplay Chris Geleplay Victor Geleplay Moses Geleplay Teta Geleplay	
	Stephen Geleplay		

Compiled
Feb. 2025

- 231 -

www.ingramcontent.com/pod-product-compliance
Lightning Source LLC
Chambersburg PA
CBHW070640150426
42811CB00050B/463